ROLL
of
NEW HAMPSHIRE SOLDIERS
at the
BATTLE of BENNINGTON
August 16, 1777

Compiled by George C. Gilmore

With

ROLL
of
NEW HAMPSHIRE MEN
at
LOUISBURG, CAPE BRETON
1745

CLEARFIELD

Roll of New Hampshire Soldiers at the Battle of Bennington, August 16, 1777
was originally published at
Manchester, New Hampshire, 1891

Roll of New Hampshire Men at Louisburg, Cape Breton, 1745
was originally published at
Concord, New Hampshire, 1896

Reprinted, two volumes in one, for
Clearfield Company by
Genealogical Publishing Company
Baltimore, Maryland
1995, 1998, 2011

ISBN 978-0-8063-4585-7

Made in the United States of America

MAJ.-GEN. JOHN STARK.

FROM THE ORIGINAL SKETCH MADE BY MISS HANNAH CROWNINSHIELD, OF SALEM, MASS.,
MAY 31, 1810.

ROLL

OF

NEW HAMPSHIRE SOLDIERS

AT THE

BATTLE OF BENNINGTON,

AUGUST 16, 1777.

COMPILED BY GEO. C. GILMORE,
MANCHESTER, N. H.

INTRODUCTION.

New Hampshire, one of the thirteen original States, contains only 9,280 square miles. One hundred and fifty-two years had come and gone since the first settlement at Dover Neck. The hardy pioneers and their descendants, poor in this world's goods, but in energy and self reliance the equal of the same number of people on the face of the earth, had pushed on into the wilderness, contending at every step, with savage Indians and wild beasts. When the Revolutionary war commenced, in 1775, there were within its borders 80,915 inhabitants.

In April, 1775, when the British soldiers held Boston, 2,000 New Hampshire men were in the ranks under the command of Stark, Reed, Prescott, and others ; and on June 17, 1,651 names appear on the rolls as taking part in the battle of Bunker Hill, 48 of them consecrating with their lives the ground on which the monument stands,— the proudest emblem of Massachusetts on her soil. The battle of Bennington, fought August 16, 1777, under the command of General John Stark with * 2,000 men, — 1,467 of them New Hampshire men, as appear by the rolls, or 73 men of every hundred, — prepared another, as Stark aptly characterizes the place, "fortunate spot" for Vermont to raise her crowning glory.

The officers are generally well known, but what of the rank and file who, in the July and August heat, marched the weary miles and dusty roads ? Even the muster or pay-rolls do not show where the men were from, and the object of this publication is mainly to make a permanent, alphabetically arranged, record of the New Hampshire men (the residence being supplied by the compiler from every available source), omitting all who died or left before, or enlisted after, August 16, 1777, from the roll, but entering the others in foot notes. The men in the Bennington campaign were enlisted for two months. The names of the towns changed, are given as they are now.

* Capt. Peter Kimball of Boscawen, who commanded a company in the battle, wrote in his diary of the campaign, " Plunder money divided to 2,250 men. "

The outline sketch of General Stark given in the frontispiece was made by Miss Crowninshield 33 years after the battle of Bennington, on very coarse paper, now yellow with age, and done with red chalk or crayon.

The State Papers, New Hampshire Revolutionary War Rolls, are the volume and page referred to in this work, where, in the left hand upper margin, the figures designate the volume and page of the original manuscript on file in the office of the Secretary of State, or Adjutant General.

MANCHESTER, N. H., July, 1891. COMPILER.

A committee appointed by the citizens of Bennington invited General Stark to visit them, and celebrate the victory of August 16, 1777, with his old companions in arms, " Sons of Liberty." The letter is dated July 22, 1809. His reply to them (in part) was as follows :

" AT MY QUARTERS, DERRYFIELD, 31st of July, 1809.

My Friends and Fellow Soldiers: — Nothing could afford me greater pleasure than to meet your brave Sons of liberty on the fortunate spot ; but, as you justly anticipate, the infirmities of old age will not permit it, for I am now more than fourscore and one years old, and the lamp of life is almost spent. I have of late had many such invitations, but was not ready, for there was not oil in the lamp. "

SALEM, Mass., June 18, 1810.

My Dear General: — The likeness my young pupil, Miss Hannah Crowninshield, took, proved to be a good one. All your friends knew it instantly. The enclosed is a copy. The original is as large as life. She is taking a copy for President Madison, and then I intend to get it engraved, and painted in oil colors. Any corrections will be accepted, as she had only one sitting. With veneration and respect,

Your sincere friend,

WILLIAM BENTLEY.

GENERAL JOHN STARK, Derryfield.

[*James Madison to the Rev. William Bentley.*]

WASHINGTON, July 8th. 1810.

Sir; I have received your favor of the second instant, accompanied by a likeness of General Stark. I thank you for both. The latter, in its execution, seems to do much credit to the talent of your pupil, that I, the more readily, confide in its likeness ; and shall place it by the side of others, whose originals are known to have inspired the General with that esteem of which they are worthy.

The circumstances related in your letter coincide with the more important anecdotes recorded of this patriot and hero, in shewing a mind made of nature's best stuff, and fashioned in a mold seldom used by her. Accept assurances of my esteem and friendly respects.

JAMES MADISON.

[John Adams to the Rev. William Bentley.]

QUINCY November 10th. 1810.

Dear Sir; I have added another to my numerous faults, in not sooner acknowledging your favor in sending me the Pears, and returning you and Mr. Endicot my best thanks for the greatful Present.

I have not given up the hope of seeing you and that young Lady (Miss Crowninshield) who flattered me with exquisite Art by representing me with the Face and Figure of a wise Man, at Quincy. I believe it is the only Portrait of me that ever was made with any appearance of Wisdom or Dignity in the Shape Air or Countenance.

Our Excellent Friend the Lieutenant Governor gave me some hopes that I might have the pleasure of seeing you here, which I earnestly desire, and if that accomplished young Lady will accompany you she will greatly increase the obligation of your obliged Friend and very humble servant,

JOHN ADAMS.

REVD. WILLIAM BENTLEY, at Salem.

The New Hampshire Legislature of 1891 made an appropriation to purchase a portrait of Gen. John Stark, and the Governor and Council appointed Ex-Gov. B. F. Prescott and George C. Gilmore a committee for that purpose.

They have made a contract with Mr. U. D. Tenney, the artist, of Concord, for an oil painting, 27x34 inch canvas, from the original likeness of the General, made by Miss Hannah Crowninshield of Salem, Mass., May 31, 1810, he then being 82 years of age.

The committee are under great obligations to Mr. Richard M. Bartleman, and Miss Mary R. Crowninshield for the loan of the original sketch, and copies of letters from President Madison and Ex-President John Adams.

NEW HAMPSHIRE SOLDIERS AT BENNINGTON

AUG. 16, 1777.

Name.	Residence.	Regiment.	Rank.	Company.	Enlisted.	Vol.	Page.
Ashley Samuel – [1]	Claremont		Col		July 18	15	141
Adams William	Londonderry	Nichols's	P	Reynolds's	20	"	201
Anderson John – [2]	"	"	Sergt	"	20	"	199
Anderson Allen	"	"	P	"	20	"	201
Applin John	Swanzey	"	P	Wright's	23	"	204
Ashley William	Winchester	"	P	"	23	"	205
Allds John – [3]	Litchfield	"	P	Ford's	20	"	207
Arbuckle William	Merrimack	"	P	"	20	"	207
Ayers Samuel – [4]	"	"	Corpl	"	20	"	206
Abbott George	Wilton	"	P	Goss's	20	"	210
Adams William – [5]	Hollis	"	P	"	20	"	209
Austin Thomas	Mason	"	P	"	20	"	209
Averill Moses	Amherst	"	P	"	20	"	210
Adams Daniel	Fitzwilliam	"	P	Stone's	21	"	218
Averill David	Jaffrey	"	P	"	21	"	217
Adams Eli	Stoddard	"	P	Parker's	19	"	221
Appleton Francis	New Ipswich	"	P	"	19	"	220
Amidon Ephraim	Chesterfield	"	P	Carleton's	22	"	223
Aiken Andrew – [6]	Chester	Stickney's	Sergt	Dearborn's	21	"	167
Allen Daniel	"	"	P	"	21	"	168
Andrews Solomon	Hillsborough	"	P	Webster's	20	"	165
Adams John	Moultonborough	"	Lieut	Taylor's	22	"	171
Atkinson Benjamin	Sandwich	"	P	"	22	"	172
Abbott Jeremiah	Pembroke	"	P	McConnell's	19	"	175
Abbott John	"	"	P	"	19	"	177
Aiken John	Bedford	"	P	"	19	"	176
Alexander James	Dunbarton	"	P	"	19	"	175
Ames Samuel		"	P	"	19	"	174
Ames Solomon		"	P	"	19	"	175

1 — Formerly of Winchester. Volunteer aid on Gen. Stark's staff.
2, 3, 4, 5, 6 — At Bunker Hill.
Atkinson, Benjamin — Kimball's Co., enlisted Aug. 24, 1777. Vol. 15, 187.

Name.	Residence.	Regiment.	Rank.	Company.	Enlisted.	Vol.	Page.
tin John		Stickney's	P	Mc. Connell's	July 19	15	175
Alexander Jabez	Henniker	"	P	Bayley's	22	"	183
Abbott Jesse	Concord	"	Sergt	Kimball's	20	"	185
Abbott John	"	"	Corpl	"	20	"	185
Abbott Elias	"	"	Fifer	"	20	"	185
Abbott Ephraim	"	"	P	"	20	"	185
Abbott Stephen — [1]	"	"	P	"	20	"	185
Abbott Ezra	"	"	P	"	20	"	185
Ambrose Benjamin	"	"	P	"	20	"	185
Ambrose Jonathan	Boscawen	"	P	"	20	"	185
Avery John	Gilmanton	"	P	N. Wilson's	22	"	195
Adams Aaron	Charlestown	Hobart's	P	Walker's	21	"	145
Allen Benjamin	"	"	P	"	21	"	145
Allen Moses	Claremont	"	P	"	21	"	144
Alexander Philip	"	"	P	Webber's	21	"	146
Ashley Martin	Walpole	"	P	"	21	"	147
Ames Stephen	Groton	"	P	Elliot's	21	"	150
Atwood Joseph	Alexandria	"	P	"	21	"	150
Aspinwall Zalman	Lebanon	"	P	Hendee's	24	"	156
Bailey Dudley — [2]	Salem	Nichols's	P	Reynolds's	20	"	200
Barr John	Londonderry	"	P	"	20	"	199
Brewster David	"	"	P	"	20	"	201
Brown Samuel — [3]	Chester	"	P	"	20	"	201
Burrows Nathaniel — [4]	Londonderry	"	P	"	20	"	199
Burrows William	"	"	P	"	20	"	200
Barney Jeffrey	Richmond	"	P	Wright's	23	"	204
Barrus Jeremiah	"	"	P	"	23	"	204
Bishop Daniel	Swanzey	"	P	"	23	"	204
Bishop Bethuel	Marlborough	"	P	"	23	"	204
Bond Asa	Winchester	"	P	"	23	"	203
Bosworth Jeremiah	Richmond	"	P	"	23	"	204
Brett Seth	Winchester	"	P	"	23	"	205
Bullock Nathan	Richmond	"	P	"	23	"	205
Burt Amasa	Winchester	"	P	"	23	"	203
Barron Samuel — [5]	Merrimack	"	P	Ford's	20	"	207
Bixby Edward — [6]	Litchfield	"	P	"	20	"	207
Bixby William	"	"	P	"	20	"	206
Blodget Joseph	Hudson	"	P	"	20	"	206
Bowers Benjamin	Merrimack	"	Lieut	"	20	"	206
Ballard Nathan	Wilton	"	Lieut	Goss's	20	"	209
Barrett Joseph	Mason	"	P	"	20	"	211
Batchelder Archelaus — [7]	Wilton	"	Sergt	"	20	"	209
Batchelder Uzziel	"	"	P	"	20	"	211
Bayley William Jr	Wilton	"	Corpl	"	20	"	209

1, 2, 3, 4, 5, 6 — At Bunker Hill.
7 — Wounded.

Name.	Residence.	Regiment.	Rank.	Company.	Enlisted.	Vol.	Page.
Blodgett Jacob – [1]	Mason	Nichols's	Ensign	Goss's	July 20	15	209
Blood Simeon	Hollis	"	P	"	20	"	209
Bowers Henry	"	"	P	"	20	"	209
Brown Eliphalet	"	"	P	"	20	"	209
Bullard Peter	Mason	"	P	"	20	"	211
Blanchard Simon	Milford	"	P	Bradford's	19	"	215
Boutell Reuben	Amherst	"	P	"	19	"	214
Bradford John	"	"	Capt	"	19	"	213
Burnham Israel	"	"	P	"	19	"	214
Burnham David	"	"	P	"	19	"	214
Burnham Jonathan – [2]	"	"	P	"	19	"	214
Bailey Abraham	Jaffrey	"	Sergt	Stone's	21	"	216
Ball Abner	Fitzwilliam	"	P	"	21	"	218
Beales Benjamin – [3]	Rindge	"	P	"	21	"	217
Bishop Samuel – [4]	Marlborough	"	P	"	21	"	218
Blodgett Jonathan	Jaffrey	"	P	"	21	"	217
Breed Thomas K	Nelson	"	P	"	21	"	217
Barrett Isaac	Stoddard	"	P	Parker's	19	"	221
Bancroft Caleb	Temple	"	P	"	19	"	220
Blair John – [5]	Peterborough	"	P	"	19	"	221
Blair William	"	"	P	"	19	"	221
Breed Allen	New Ipswich	"	P	"	19	"	219
Breed Allen Jr	"	"	P	"	19	"	219
Brockway Ephraim	Stoddard	"	P	"	19	"	221
Brockway Asa	Washington	"	P	"	19	"	221
Brown Ephraim	Temple	"	Corpl	"	19	"	219
Byam Benjamin	"	"	Sergt	"	19	"	219
Baldwin Daniel	Chesterfield	"	P	Carleton's	22	"	225
Belding Elisha – [6]	Hinsdale	"	P	"	22	"	224
Bingham Theodorus	Chesterfield	"	P	"	22	"	224
Blanchard Daniel	Westmoreland	"	P	"	22	"	225
Britton William	"	"	P	"	22	"	224
Brown Daniel – [7]	"	"	P	"	22	"	225
Brown Nehemiah – [8]	"	"	P	"	22	"	225
Brown Jesse	"	"	P	"	22	"	224
Bebee Peter	Gilsum	"	P	Mack's	22	"	226
Bond David	"	"	P	"	22	"	226
Boynton John Jr	"	"	Fifer	"	22	"	226
Bragg Ebenezer	"	"	P	"	22	"	226
Bragg Nicholas	"	"	P	"	22	"	226
Barker Benjamin	Pelham	"	Corpl	J. Wilson's	21	"	228
Barker Richard	"	"	P	"	21	"	229
Bolton William	Windham	"	P	"	21	"	229
Bachelor Jonathan		Stickney's	P	Dearborn's	19	"	169

1, 2, 3, 4, 5, 6 — At Bunker Hill.
7, 8 — Wounded.

Name.	Residence.	Regiment.	Rank.	Company.	Enlisted.	Vol.	Page.
Bagley John	Candia	Stickney's	P	Dearborn's	July 19	15	169
Blake John	"	"	P	"	21	"	168
Blaisdell Isaac	Chester	"	P	"	19	"	169
Brown Joseph	"	"	P	"	19	"	169
Brown William	"	"	P	"	19	"	169
Barber Robert	Salisbury	"	P	Webster's	20	"	165
Booth William	Hillsborough	"	Corpl	"	20	"	164
Burwash Nathaniel	Andover	"	P	"	20	"	164
Bean Josiah	Sandwich	"	Lieut	Taylor's	22	"	171
Bean Benjamin	"	"	P	"	22	"	172
Bean John	Moultonborough	"	Sergt	"	22	"	171
Boynton David	"	"	P	"	22	"	173
Bryen John	Sanbornton	"	P	"	22	"	171
Brown Daniel	Moultonborough	"	Corpl	"	22	"	171
Brown Eliphalet	Sanbornton	"	P	"	22	"	173
Bryant Robert	Meredith	"	Ensign	"	22	"	171
Burleigh Thomas	Sandwich	"	P	"	22	"	172
Barker James	"	"	P	McConnell's	19	"	177
Barnet John	Bedford	"	P	"	19	"	176
Bell John	"	"	P	"	19	"	175
Betle Benjamin	"	"	P	"	19	"	177
Burns Robert	Bedford	"	Sergt	"	19	"	174
Batchelder Nathaniel	Loudon	"	P	Sias's	20	"	180
Batchelder Richard	"	"	P	"	20	"	180
Batchelder Phinehas	"	"	P	"	20	"	180
Batchelder Thomas	"	"	P	"	20	"	179
Bean Benjamin	Bow	"	Corpl	"	20	"	179
Blaisdell Ezra	Loudon	"	P	"	20	"	180
Blanchard David	Canterbury	"	Sergt	"	20	"	179
Bayley Joshua	Hopkinton	"	Capt	Bayley's	20	"	182
Bayley Phinehas	"	"	P	"	22	"	183
Bayley Solomon	"	"	P	"	22	"	183
Bowman Jonas	Henniker	"	Lieut	"	21	"	182
Bowman Zaduc	"	"	P	"	22	"	183
Brown Ensley – [1]	Hopkinton	"	P	"	22	"	183
Burbank John	"	"	Corpl	"	21	"	182
Burbank Caleb	"	"	P	"	22	"	183
Beedle Thomas	Boscawen	"	P	Kimball's	20	"	185
Blanchard Peter	Concord	"	P	"	20	"	185
Bradley Philbrick	"	"	P	"	20	"	186
Burbank David – [2]	Boscawen	"	Corpl	"	20	"	185
Burbank Wells	"	"	P	"	20	"	185
Bayley Miles – [3]	"	"	P	Clark's	21	"	189
Bales John	Deering	"	P	"	21	"	188

1, 2 — At Bunker Hill.
3 — On roll taken (prisoner) Aug. 14.

Name.	Residence.	Regiment.	Rank.	Company.	Enlisted.	Vol.	Page.
Beard William – [1]	New Boston	Stickney's	Ensign	Clark's	July 21	15	188
Blanchard Josiah	"	"	P	"	21	"	189
Bradford Benjamin	Deering	"	Lieut	"	21	"	188
Bradford William	"	"	Sergt	"	21	"	188
Burnham Nathaniel	Lyndeborough	"	P	"	21	"	188
Burnham Stephen	"	"	P	"	21	"	189
Butterfield Oliver	Francestown	"	P	"	21	"	189
Balch Nathaniel	Wakefield	"	P	Gilman's	20	"	191
Berry Samuel	"	"	P	"	20	"	192
Berry John B	"	"	P	"	20	"	192
Brown John	"	"	P	"	20	"	191
Bryant James	"	"	P	"	20	"	192
Batchelder Jethro	Barnstead	"	P	N. Wilson's	22	"	194
Benjamin Judah	Claremont	Hobart's	P	Walker's	21	"	145
Bailey Jesse	Newport	"	P	Webber's	21	"	147
Beckwith Martin	Marlow	"	P	"	21	"	147
Bingham Nathan	Lempster	"	P	"	21	"	147
Booth Joshua	"	"	P	"	21	"	147
Boynton Andrew	Marlow	"	P	"	21	"	146
Brown Abraham Jr	Alstead	"	P	"	21	"	147
Brown Aaron	"	"	P	"	21	"	147
Buel Daniel	Newport	"	P	"	21	"	147
Burroughs John Jr	Alstead	"	Sergt	"	21	"	146
Burroughs Elijah	"	"	P	"	21	"	147
Blanchard Isaac	Plymouth	"	P	Elliot's	21	"	150
Blodgett James	"	"	P	"	21	"	150
Blodgett Jonathan	Rumney	"	P	"	21	"	150
Brainard Chileab	Campton	"	P	"	21	"	149
Brown Josiah	Plymouth	"	P	"	21	"	149
Bussell John	Hill	"	Corpl	"	21	"	149
Butterfield Zachariah – [2]	Rumney	"	Corpl	"	21	"	149
Barron Jonathan	Haverhill	"	P	Post's	24	"	153
Baxter John	Lyme	"	P	"	24	"	153
Bayley Abijah	Haverhill	"	P	"	24	"	152
Bowles Charles	"	"	P	"	24	"	153
Bugbee Timothy	Lyme	"	P	"	24	"	153
Baldwin Jabez	Lebanon	"	Corpl	Hendee's	23	"	155
Bartlett Nathaniel	Canaan	"	P	"	23	"	157
Basford Joseph	Orange	"	P	"	23	"	157
Bingham Elisha	Enfield	"	Corpl	"	23	"	155
Bliss Azariah Jr	Lebanon	"	P	"	23	"	156
Bliss Josiah	"	"	P	"	23	"	156

1 — At Bunker Hill.
2 — Killed.
    Bohonnon Andrew, Lieutenant, Webster's Co.; Bohonnon Jacob, Private, Webster's Co.; Bayley George, Private, Webster's Co.; Brottlebank Daniel, Private, Webster's Co , — enlisted August 25, 1777. Vol. 15, 164.
    Burbank Nathaniel, Kimball's Co., enlisted August 24, 1777. Vol. 15, 187.

2

Name.	Residence.	Regiment.	Rank.	Company.	Enlisted.	Vol.	Page.
Blunt Cornelius	Plainfield	Hobart's	P	Hendee's	July 23	15	155
Brewer Ebenezer	Cornish	"	P	"	23	"	156
Bridgman Abel	Hanover	"	P	"	23	"	157
Bullock Simeon	Grafton	"	P	"	23	"	157
Casey John – ¹	Epsom		Clerk		18	"	141
Caldwell Joseph	Windham	Nichols's	P	Reynolds's	20	"	201
Campbell John	"	"	P	"	20	"	200
Campbell Samuel	"	"	P	"	20	"	200
Carr Thomas	Chester	"	P	"	20	"	200
Cheney Jonathan	Londonderry	"	P	"	20	"	200
Cheney Nathaniel	"	"	P	"	20	"	200
Clark David	"	"	Corpl	"	20	"	199
Colby Isaac	"	"	P	"	20	"	199
Conant Joshua – ²	"	"	P	"	20	"	201
Cunningham Archibald – ³	Francestown	"	P	"	20	"	200
Carpenter William	Swanzey	"	P	Wright's	23	"	205
Cook James	Richmond	"	P	"	23	"	204
Cummins Ephraim	Swanzey	"	P	"	23	"	204
Cowin William – ⁴	Merrimack	"	P	Ford's	20	"	207
Cross Joseph	Hudson	"	P	"	20	"	206
Cutter Seth	"	"	P	"	20	"	206
Campbell John – ⁵	Hollis	"	P	Goss's	20	"	209
Conick John	Brookline	"	P	"	20	"	209
Cram Ebenezer	Wilton	"	P	"	20	"	211
Cram Zebulon	"	"	P	"	20	"	211
Cole Nathan	Amherst	"	Corpl	Bradford's	19	"	213
Crosby William	"	"	P	"	19	"	214
Crosby Stephen – ⁶	"	"	P	"	19	"	214
Curtice Jacob – ⁷	"	"	Corpl	"	19	"	213
Curtice Stephen	"	"	P	"	19	"	213
Curtice Isaac	"	"	P	"	19	"	214
Curtice Lemuel	"	"	P	"	19	"	215
Converse Robert	Marlborough	"	P	Stone's	21	"	218
Cragin Benjamin	Temple	"	Lieut	Parker's	19	"	219
Cunningham Samuel	Peterborough	"	Lieut	"	19	"	219
Carleton Kimball	Chesterfield	"	Capt	Carleton's	22	"	223
Cobleigh Jonathan	"	"	P¹¹	"	22	"	225
Cobb Simon	Westmoreland	"	P¹	"	22	"	224
Cole Jonathan	"	"	Corpl	"	22	"	223
Collins Nathaniel	Hinsdale	"	P	"	22	"	225
Converse Samuel D	Chesterfield	"	P	"	22	"	224
Clark Cephas	Keene	"	P	Mack's	22	"	226

1 — In the House of Representatives July 19, 1777 : Voted " That Mr. John Casey be appointed Clerk to Genˡ Stark, and that he be paid the same wages as a Lieutenant in the Continental army during his continuance in the service " at Bunker Hill.
2 — Wounded ; died September 10, 1777.
3 — Wounded ; died August 28, 1777.
4, 5, 6, 7, — At Bunker Hill.

Name.	Residence.	Regiment.	Rank.	Company.	Enlisted.	Vol.	Page.
Cook Ebenezer – [1]	Keene	Nichols's	Sergt. Major.	Mack's	July 22	15	226
Campbell David	Windham	"	P	J. Wilson's	21	"	228
Coburn Edward	Pelham	"	P	"	21	"	228
Cole Eliphalet	"	"	P	"	21	"	228
Corliss Emerson – [2]	Salem	"	P	"	21	"	228
Chase Josiah	Canterbury	Stickney's	S'rgeon			"	163
Clements William	Hopkinton	"	Q. M.			"	163
Cammet John	Candia	"	P	Dearborn's	21	"	168
Cass Joseph	"	"	Sergt	"	21	"	167
Chase Jacob	Chester	"	P	"	21	"	168
Clay John	Candia	"	P	"	21	"	169
Clifford Israel	"	"	P	"	21	"	167
Clifford Anthony	"	"	P	"	21	"	168
Colby Enoch	"	"	P	"	21	"	169
Currier David – [3]	Chester	"	P	"	21	"	169
Colby Rowell	Salisbury	"	P	Webster's	20	"	165
Calley Thomas	Sanbornton	"	P	Taylor's	22	"	171
Cate Elisha	"	"	P	"	22	"	171
Cate Simeon	"	"	P	"	22	"	173
Carr Samuel	Meredith	"	P	"	22	"	173
Chamberlin Ephraim	Alton	"	P	"	22	"	172
Clark Nicholas	Sanbornton	"	Sergt	"	22	"	171
Clark Satchell	"	"	P	"	22	"	171
Clements Richard	Moultonborough	"	P	"	22	"	172
Cook Ebenezer	"	"	P	"	22	"	172
Critchet Thomas	Sanbornton	"	Corpl	"	22	"	171
Carr Samuel	Goffstown	"	P	McConnell's	19	"	175
Church John	Dunbarton	"	P	"	19	"	176
Cilley Jonathan	Seabrook	"	P	"	19	"	174
Colby Hezekiah	Dunbarton	"	P	"	19	"	176
Colby Joseph	Weare	"	P	"	19	"	175
Collins Daniel	"	"	P	"	19	"	177
Carr Joseph	Canterbury	"	P	Sias's	20	"	179
Carter Samuel	Loudon	"	P	"	20	"	180
Chamberlin William	"	"	Sergt	"	20	"	179
Clough Joseph	Canterbury	"	P	"	20	"	180
Clough David	Bow	"	P	"	20	"	180
Cross John	Canterbury	"	P	"	20	"	179
Currier Reuben	Bow	"	P	"	20	"	180
Curry Thomas	Canterbury	"	P	"	20	"	179
Colby Levi	Hopkinton	"	P	Bayley's	22	"	183
Colby David	"	"	P	"	22	"	183
Corbet Josiah	"	"	P	"	21	"	183
Currier Henry	"	"	P	"	22	"	183
Carter Daniel	Boscawen	"	P	Kimball's	20	"	186
Chase Abner	Warner	"	P	"	20	"	186

1, 2, 3 — At Bunker Hill.

Name.	Residence.	Regiment.	Rank.	Company.	Enlisted.	Vol.	Page.
Corser Asa – [1]	Boscawen	Stickney's	Drum	Kimball's	July 20	15	185
Corser Jonathan	"	"	P	"	20	"	186
Corser David	"	"	P	"	20	"	186
Cavander Charles	Greenfield	"	Corpl	Clark's	21	"	188
Clark Peter	Lyndeborough	"	Capt	"	21	"	188
Cochran Elijah	New Boston	"	P	"	21	"	189
Cram Benjamin Jr	Lyndeborough	"	P	"	21	"	189
Clark John	Barnstead	"	Sergt	N. Wilson's	22	"	194
Clough Simon	Gilmanton	"	P	"	22	"	194
Chamberlin Jacob	Alton	"	P	"	22	"	195
Chase Solomon	Cornish	Hobart's	S'rgeon		25	"	142
Call James	Charlestown	"	P	Walker's	21	"	145
Clark Joseph	Claremont	"	Sergt	"	21	"	143
Clark Dan	"	"	P	"	21	"	145
Cook Oliver	"	"	P	"	21	"	144
Cross John – [2]	Charlestown	"	Sergt	"	21	"	143
Church Jabez	Campton	"	Sergt	Elliot's	21	"	149
Clark John	Hill	"	P	"	21	"	150
Clifford Zachariah	Rumney	"	P	"	21	"	150
Clifford Jonathan	Hill	"	P	"	21	"	150
Colby Eli –[3]	Alexandria	"	P	"	21	"	150
Crawford Thomas	Hill	"	Sergt. Major	"	21	"	149
Cross Daniel	Rumney	"	P	"	21	"	150
Case Zenas	Piermont	"	P	Post's	24	"	153
Clark John	Landaff	"	P	"	24	"	153
Clark John	Orford	"	P	"	24	"	153
Clark Joseph	Haverhill	"	Corpl	"	24	"	152
Clark Edward	"	"	P	"	24	"	153
Cleaveland Elisha	Bath	"	P	"	24	"	153
Cook Charles	Piermont	"	Sergt	"	24	"	152
Cady Nicholas	Cornish	"	P	Hendee's	23	"	155
Chase Daniel	"	"	Lieut	"	23	"	155
Clark Josiah	Canaan	"	P	"	23	"	157
Colburn Jacob	Lebanon	"	P	"	23	"	156
Colburn Asa	"	"	P	"	23	"	156
Colton Caleb	Grantham	"	P	"	23	"	156
Colton Stephen	"	"	P	"	23	"	156
Cooper Sherman	Croydon	"	P	"	23	"	156
Cooper Joel	"	"	P	"	23	"	156
Corey Isaac	Plainfield	"	P	"	23	"	155
Corliss Elisha	Orange	"	Fifer	"	23	"	155
Cummings Benjamin	Cornish	"	Corpl	"	23	"	155
Currier Peter	Plainfield	"	P	"	23	"	155

1, 2 — At Bunker Hill.
3 — Killed.

Calef William, Webster's Co., enlisted Aug. 25. Vol. 15, 165.
Cooley John, Taylor's Co., discharged Aug. 10. Vol. 15, 173.
Corser Nathan, Corser William, Kimball's Co., enlisted Aug. 24. Vol. 15, 187.
Cook Thomas, Elliot's Co., died Aug. 7. Vol. 15, 149.

Name.	Residence.	Regiment.	Rank.	Company.	Enlisted.	Vol.	Page
Cutler Knights	Plainfield	Hobart's	P	Hendee's	July 23	15	155
Cutler Hodges	"	"	P	"	23	"	156
Dickey Mathew	Londonderry	Nichols's	Corpl	Reynolds's	20	"	199
Dickey Adam	"	"	P	"	20	"	201
Davis Ebenezer	Rindge	"	P	Wright's	23	"	204
Dakin Justus	Hudson	"	Corpl	Ford's	20	"	206
Danforth Solomon	Merrimack	. "	P	"	20	"	207
Davis Gideon	"	"	P	"	20	"	207
Dascomb James	Wilton	"	P	Goss's	20	"	211
Dutton Roger – ¹	Amherst	"	P	Bradford's	19	"	213
Darling Eliakim	Rindge	"	P	Stone's	21	"	217
Davis William	"	"	P	"	21	"	217
Davis John Jr	Jaffrey	"	P	"	21	"	217
Day Noah	Nelson	"	Corpl	"	21	"	216
Dean John	Rindge	"	P	"	21	"	216
Dean James	Marlborough	"	P	"	21	"	218
Drury Needham	Temple	"	P	Parker's	19	"	220
Dunn Benjamin	Stoddard	"	P	"	19	"	221
Dutton Abel	"	"	P	"	19	"	221
Daggit Simeon	Westmoreland	"	P	Carleton's	22	"	224
Dolfe Matthew		"	P	Mack's	22	"	226
Durant Joshua	Keene	"	P	"	22	"	226
Dwinell Jonathan	"	"	P	"	22	"	227
Davidson Jesse	Windham	"	P	J. Wilson's	21	"	228
Dearborn Stephen	Chester	Stickney's	Capt	Dearborn's	19	"	167
Dearborn Ebenezer	"	"	P	"	19	"	168
Dearborn Sherburn	"	"	P	"	19	"	169
Dearborn Samuel	Candia	"	P	"	19	"	169
Dearborn Thomas	"	"	Sergt	"	21	"	167
Dinsmore Robert	Chester	"	P	"	21	"	169
Davis Francis	Warner	"	P	Webster's	20	"	165
Dresser Asa	Hillsborough	"	P	"	20	"	165
Danford Jonathan	Meredith	"	P	Taylor's	22	"	173
Danford Thomas Jr	"	"	P	"	22	"	173
Dockam Thomas	Meredith	"	P	"	22	"	173
Drake Ephraim	Moultonborough	"	P	"	22	"	172
Davis Zebulon	Allenstown	"	P	McConnell's	19	"	175
Davis Malachi	"	"	P	"	19	"	175
Dunlap Samuel	Goffstown	"	P	"	19	"	175
Durgen Gersham	Allenstown	"	P	"	19	"	177
Duston Paul	Weare	"	P	"	19	"	177
Dearborn Nathaniel	Canterbury	"	P	Sias's	20	"	180
Dow John	Bow	"	P	"	20	"	180
Dusten James	Henniker	"	P	Bayley's	22	"	183
Danforth William	Boscawen	"	Sergt	Kimball's	20	"	185
Danforth Elkanah	Concord	"	P	"	20	"	186

1 — At Bunker Hill.

3

Name.	Residence.	Regiment.	Rank.	Company.	Enlisted.	Vol.	Page.
Danforth Simeon — [1]	Concord	Stickney's	P	Kimball's	July 20	15	186
Davis Nathan — [2]	Boscawen	"	Sergt	"	20	"	185
Dimond Reuben	Concord	"	P	"	20	"	186
Dodge Nehemiah	New Boston	"	P	Clark's	21	"	189
Dodge Jacob	" "	"	P	"	21	"	189
Duncklee Hezekiah	Lyndeborough	"	P	"	21	"	189
Dutton Ezra — [3]	"	"	Corpl	"	21	"	188
Dutton Jacob — [4]	"	"	Fifer	"	21	"	188
Dearborn Simeon Jr	Wakefield	"	P	Gilman's	20	"	191
Doe Simeon		"	P	"	20	"	191
Dean Benjamin W	Gilmanton	"	P	N Wilson's	22	"	195
Dudley Daniel	"	"	Corpl	"	22	"	194
Durgen Winthrop		"	P	"	22	"	195
Dunfee James	Claremont	Hobart's	P	Walker's	21	"	144
Deming Martin — [5]	Walpole	"	Fifer	Webber's	21	"	146
Dennison Jedediah	"	"	P	"	21	"	147
Debbil Alexander — [6]	"	"	P	"	21	"	147
Dudley Daniel	Newport	"	P	"	21	"	147
Davis Thomas	Piermont	"	P	Post's	24	"	153
Derby Simeon	Orford	"	P	"	24	"	153
Ellis Timothy	Keene	Nichols's	Major		23	"	198
Eviston George	"		P	Reynolds's	20	"	199
Elgar Waitstill	Winchester	"	P	Wright's	23	"	205
Ellis John	Richmond	"	Sergt	"	23	"	203
Ellis John	Winchester	"	P	"	23	"	204
Emerson Oliver	Litchfield	"	Sergt	Ford's	20	"	206
Emerson Seth	Merrimack	"	P	"	20	"	207
Elliot Oliver	Mason	"	P	Goss's	20	"	211
Elliot Samuel	"	"	P	"	20	"	211
Elliot David	"	"	P	"	20	"	211
Elliot Amos	Amherst	"	Corpl	Bradford's	19	"	213
Ellinwood Jedediah	"	"	P	"	19	"	214
Everdon John	"	"	P	"	19	"	214
Everett John	Temple	"	P	Parker's	19	"	220
Emmons Noah	Chesterfield	"	Corpl	Carleton's	22	"	223
Evans Elzy	Hinsdale	"	P	"	22	"	223
Emerson Nathaniel	Candia	Stickney's	Lieut Colonel		23	"	161
Evans Edward	Plymouth	"	Adjt		23	"	161
Eaton Benjamin	Candia	"	P	Dearborn's	21	"	169
Elliot John	Chester	"	Drum'r	"	21	"	170
Elliot Jacob — [7]	"	"	P	"	21	"	168
Emerson Moses	Candia	"	P	"	21	"	169
Elkins Moses	Salisbury	"	P	Webster's	20	"	165
Ellsworth Aaron	Sanbornton	"	P	Taylor's	22	"	173

1, 2, 3, 4, 5, 6 — At Bunker Hill.
7 — Wounded.

Name	Residence.	Regiment.	Rank.	Company.	Enlisted.	Vol.	Page.
Eaton Enoch	Goffstown	Stickney's	P	McConnell's	July 19	15	174
Eaton Samuel	Weare	"	P	"	19	"	176
Emerson William	"	"	P	"	19	"	177
Evans George – [1]	Allenstown	"	P	"	19	"	175
Eastman, Samuel – [2]	Henniker	"	P	Bayley's	22	"	183
Eastman Jonathan	"	"	Corpl	"	22	"	182
Eastman Enoch	Hopkinton	"	P	"	21	"	182
Eaton Ebenezer	"	"	Corpl	"	22	"	182
Emerson Moses	"	"	P	"	22	"	183
Elliot Benjamin	Concord	"	P	Kimball's	20	"	186
Eaton James	Goffstown	"	P	Clark's	21	"	189
Ellinwood Benjamin	Lyndeborough	"	P	"	21	"	188
Ellis Barnabas	Middleton	"	P	Gilman's	20	"	192
Emerson Benjamin	Barnstead	"	P	N. Wilson's	22	"	195
Ellis Joseph	Claremont	Hobart's	Lieut	Walker's	21	"	143
Eayrs Christopher	Acworth	"	P	"	21	"	144
Eastman Philip – [3]	Walpole	"	Sergt	Webber's	21	"	146
Eastman Samuel	Marlow	"	P	"	21	"	146
Elliot Edmund	Thornton	"	Capt	Elliot's	21	"	149
Emmons Benjamin	Hill	"	Ensign	"	21	"	149
Easterbrooks Samuel	Lebanon	"	Ensign	Hendee's	23	"	155
Emerson Enoch	Croydon	"	Corpl	"	23	"	155
Fitch Thaddeus – [4]	Amherst	Nichols's	Q M		24	"	198
Fellows William	"	"	P	Reynolds's	20	"	199
Ferguson John – [5]	Pelham	"	P	"	20	"	200
Field Waitstill – [6]	Winchester	"	P	Wright's	23	"	205
Follet, Benjamin	Swanzey	"	P	"	23	"	204
Franklin Ichabod	Winchester	"	P	"	23	"	204
Fuller Jesse	Swanzey	"	P	"	23	"	204
Fears Humphrey	"	"	P	Ford's	20	"	206
Fisk Ebenezer		"	P	"	20	"	207
Ford James – [7]	Hudson	"	Capt	"	20	"	206
French Joseph	Nashua	"	Lieut	"	20	"	206
Farrington Phinehas	Wilton	"	P	Goss's	20	"	211
Fay Daniel	Mason	"	Sergt	"	20	"	209
Fisk Simeon	"	"	P	"	20	"	211
Foster Isaac	Wilton	"	P	"	20	"	211
French Jonathan	Hollis	"	P	"	20	"	209
Fuller Joseph		"	P	"	20	"	211

1, 2, 4, 5, 6 — At Bunker Hill.
3 — Wounded; died August 21, 1777.
   Emery William, lieutenant in Webster's Co., discharged August 15, 1777, on account of sickness. Vol. 15, 164.
   Elkins Abel, Webster's Co., enlisted August 25, 1777. Vol. 15, 166.
   Eastman Jeremiah, Kimball's Co., enlisted August 24, 1777. Vol. 15, 181.
   Evans John, Sias's Company, enlisted August 25, 1777. Vol. 15, 181.
7 — At Bunker Hill; wounded at Bennington.

Name.	Residence.	Regiment.	Rank.	Company.	Enlisted.	Vol.	Page.
Farnham Joseph	Amherst	Nichols's	Lieut	Bradford's	July 19	15	213
Farwell Richard	Nelson	"	P	Stone's	21	"	217
Farwell Absalom	"	"	P	"	21	"	217
French James	Jaffrey	"	P	"	21	"	217
French John	Nelson	"	P	"	21	"	217
Fletcher Peter	New Ipswich	"	P	Parker's	19	"	220
Foster James	Temple	"	P	"	19	"	220
Foster Daniel	"	"	P	"	19	"	220
Farr Jonathan Jr – 1	Chesterfield	"	P	Carleton's	22	"	224
Farr Daniel	"	"	Sergt	"	22	"	223
Farr Charles	"	"	P	"	22	"	223
Farr William	"	"	P	"	22	"	223
Farr Jacob Jr	"	"	P	"	22	"	225
Fisk Aaron	"	"	P	"	22	"	224
Frost Joshua	Hinsdale	"	P	"	22	"	225
Fields Moses	Surry	"	Lieut	Mack's	22	"	226
Fuller Joshua – 2	"	"	P	"	22	"	227
Fuller Samuel	"	"	Sergt	"	22	"	226
Fellows Benjamin	Candia	Stickney's	Corpl	Dearborn's	21	"	167
Fogg Stephen	Raymond	"	P	"	21	"	168
Fogg Samuel	"	"	P	"	21	"	169
Fox Sinclair	"	"	P	"	21	"	169
Fuller Benjamin	Chester	"	P	"	21	"	169
Fellows·Joseph	Andover	"	P	Webster's	20	"	165
Fifield Abraham	Salisbury	"	Sergt	"	20	"	164
Foster Jonathan	"	"	Fifer	"	20	"	164
Farrah Isaac	Meredith	"	P	Taylor's	22	"	173
Folsom Nicholas	"	"	P	"	22	"	173
Folsom John	Sanbornton	"	Corpl	"	22	"	171
Farmer David – 3	Manchester	"	P	McConnell's	19	"	176
Felch Nicholas	Seabrook	"	P	"	19	"	174
Ferren Ebenezer	Goffstown	"	Sergt	"	19	"	174
Forrest William	Canterbury	"	P	Sias's	20	"	181
Foster Ephraim	Bow	"	Ensign	"	20	"	179
Foster Jonathan	Canterbury	"	Sergt	"	20	"	179
Farnham Timothy	Hopkinton	"	Lieut	Bayley's	22	"	182
French Daniel	"	"	P	"	22	"	183
Farnham Theodore	Concord	"	Corpl	Kimball's	20	"	185
Fisk Ephraim	"	"	P	"	20	"	186
Fisk Ephraim Jr	"	"	P	"	20	"	186

1, 3— At Bunker Hill.

2 — At Bunker Hill; killed at Bennington.

Fifield Jonathan, Fifield John, Fifield Joseph, Fifield Edward, Webster's Co., of Salisbury; enlisted August 25, 1777. Vol. 15, 165.

Flanders John, Flanders Joseph, Flanders David, Flanders Ezekiel, Kimball's Co, of Boscawen; enlisted August 24, 1777. Vol. 15, 187.

Name.	Residence.	Regiment.	Rank.	Company.	Enlisted.	Vol.	Page.
Flanders Abner	Concord	Stickney's	Sergt	Kimball's	July 20	15	185
Flanders Jesse	Boscawen	"	P	"	20	"	186
Flood Richard – [1]	Concord	"	Corpl	"	20	"	185
French James	Boscawen	"	P	"	20	"	186
Ferson Robert	Deering	"	P	Clark's	21	"	189
Fisher Nathan	Francestown	"	Sergt	"	21	"	188
Frost Nicholas	Middleton	"	P	Gilman's	20	"	192
Frost Wentworth		"	P	"	20	"	192
Fullerton James	Wolfeborough	"	P	"	20	"	192
Fifield Samuel	Gilmanton	"	P	N Wilson's	22	"	194
Flanders Joseph	"	"	P	"	22	"	195
Flanders Ezekiel		"	Sergt	"	22	"	194
Fox John	Gilmanton	"	P	"	22	"	194
Farnsworth Oliver	Charlestown	Hobart's	P	Walker's	21	"	144
Fielding Ebenezer	Claremont	"	P	"	21	"	144
Ford Daniel	"	"	Corpl	"	21	"	143
Fuller Amasa	"	"	P	"	21	"	144
Fletcher Jonathan	Marlow	"	P	Webber's	21	"	147
Fletcher Samuel	Alstead	"	P	"	21	"	147
Farley Samuel	Groton	"	Sergt	Elliot's	21	"	149
Fellows John	Hill	"	P	"	21	"	150
Fox Uriah	Campton	"	P	"	21	"	149
Fuller Samuel	Thornton	"	P	"	21	"	149
Fairfield John	Lyme	"	Corpl	Post's	24	"	152
Ford Hezekiah	Piermont	"	P	"	24	"	153
Ford Paul	"	"	P	"	24	"	153
Ford Job	"	"	P	"	24	"	153
Fitch Samuel	Cornish	"	P	Hendee's	23	"	156
Fuller Lemuel	Lebanon	"	P	"	23	"	156
Gregg William	Londonderry	Nichols's	Lieut. Colonel	"	23	"	198
Gregg Ephraim	"	"	P	Reynolds's	20	"	201
Griffin Thomas	Sandown	"	Fifer	"	20	"	199
Green Joseph – [2]	Swanzey	"	P	Wright's	23	"	204
Gage Phinehas	Pelham	"	P	Ford's	20	"	207
Gibson James – [3]	Nashua	"	P	"	20	"	206
Gould Silas	Amherst	"	P	"	20	"	207
Goss John – [4]	Hollis	"	Capt	Goss's	20	"	209
Greeley John – [5]	Wilton	"	P	"	20	"	211
Gilbert Laraford	Amherst	"	P	Bradford's	19	"	214
Gilmore James – [6]	"	"	Sergt	"	19	"	213
Goodrich Allen	"	"	P	"	19	"	213
Green David	"	"	P	"	19	"	213
Gilmore Robert	Jaffrey	"	P	Stone's	21	"	217
Gould Stephen – [7]	Amherst	"	P	"	21	"	217
Greenwood William	Dublin	"	P	"	21	"	217

1, 2, 3, 4, 5, 6, 7 — At Bunker Hill.

Name.	Residence.	Regiment.	Rank.	Company.	Enlisted.	Vol.	Page.
Gilbert Abel	Westmoreland	Nichols's	P	Carleton's	July 22	15	225
Glazier David	"	"	P	"	22	"	225
Grandy Bazaleel	Hinsdale	"	Sergt	"	22	"	223
Gleason Job	Surry	"	P	Mack's	22	"	226
Gutridge Benjamin	"	"	P	"	22	"	226
Gage David – 1	Pelham	"	Sergt	J Wilson's	21	"	228
Gould Noah	"	"	P	"	21	"	229
Gregg David – 2	Windham	"	Ensign	"	21	"	228
Gutterson Josiah	Pelham	"	P	"	21	"	229
Gordon Josiah – 3	Raymond	Stickney's	P	Dearborn's	21	"	169
Griffin Nathaniel	Chester	"	P	"	21	"	167
Gibson James – 4	Hillsborough	"	P	Webster's	20	"	165
Gibson John	"	"	P	"	20	"	165
Gould Robert	Warner	"	Sergt	"	20	"	164
Gale Daniel – 5	Sanbornton	"	P	Taylor's	22	"	171
Gilman Caleb	Sandwich	"	P	"	22	"	172
Glidden John	"	"	P	"	22	"	172
Goldsmith John	"	"	P	"	22	"	171
Goldsmith John Jr	"	"	P	"	22	"	172
Gordon Enoch	Meredith	"	P	"	22	"	172
Gault Matthew	Pembroke	"	Drum	McConnell's	19	"	174
Garvin Ephraim	Bow	"	P	"	19	"	175
Gay James	Pembroke	"	Sergt	"	19	"	174
Gilmore Robert	Goffstown	"	Lieut	"	19	"	174
Gilmore John	"	"	P	"	19	"	176
Griffin Theophilus	Manchester	"	P	"	19	"	176
Glines Richard	Loudon	"	P	Sias's	20	"	179
Gile Joshua	Henniker	"	Sergt	Bayley's	22	"	182
Gould Christopher	Hopkinton	"	P	"	22	"	182
Gordon Amos	"	"	P	"	22	"	182
Gage Solomon	Concord	"	P	Kimball's	20	"	187
George David	"	"	P	"	20	"	187
Glines Israel	"	"	P	"	20	"	186
Greenfield Charles	Boscawen	"	P	"	20	"	186
Glover Henry – 6	New Boston	"	Sergt	Clark's	21	"	188
Gregg John – 7	" "	"	P	"	21	"	189
Gregg Reuben	" "	"	P	"	21	"	189
Grimes Francis	Deering	"	P .	"	21	"	189
Gilman Jeremiah	Wakefield	"	Capt	Gilman's	20	"	191
Gilman Benjamin	"	"	P	"	20	"	191
Gould Jeremiah	Wolfeborough	"	P	"	20	"	192
Gilman Peter	Gilmanton	"	Sergt	N Wilson's	22	"	191
Gilman Dudley	"	"	Corpl	"	22	"	194

1, 3, 4, 6, 7 — At Bunker Hill.
2 — At Bunker Hill; wounded at Bennington.
5 — Wounded.

Name.	Residence.	Regiment.	Rank.	Company.	Enlisted.	Vol	Page.
Gilman Edward Jr	Gilmanton	Stickney's	P	N Wilson's	July 22	15	194
Gleason Windsor	Charlestown	Hobart's	P	Walker's	21	"	143
Grannis Edward	Claremont	"	P	"	21	"	145
Grendel Daniel	Sunapee	"	Corpl	"	21	"	143
Gee Luman	Marlow	"	P	Webber's	21	"	147
Gilman Joshua – 1	Walpole	"	P	"	21	"	147
Grant Peter	Lyme	"	Sergt	Post's	24	"	152
Gallup Thomas Jr	Plainfield	"	Sergt	Hendee's	23	"	155
Griswold Jeremiah	Lebanon	"	P	"	23	"	156
Hastings Joseph		Nichols's	Corpl	Reynolds's	20	"	199
Hobbs Joseph	Londonderry	"	P	"	20	"	201
Houston William	"	"	P	"	20	"	199
Humphrey James	"	"	P	"	20	"	200
Hughs John	"	"	Ensign	"	20	"	199
Hatch John	Winchester	"	P	Wright's	23	"	204
Hazen Benjamin	Swanzey	"	Fifer	"	23	"	203
Healey Samuel	Winchester	"	Sergt	"	23	"	203
Heaton James	Swanzey	"	Ensign	"	23	"	203
Hicks Samuel	Richmond	"	Corpl	"	23	"	203
Hicks Eliphalet	"	"	P	"	23	"	204
Hicks Simeon	"	"	P	"	23	"	205
Holmes Joseph	Swanzey	"	Corpl	"	23	"	203
Holmes Stetson	Winchester	"	P	"	23	"	205
Houghton Edward	"	"	Corpl	"	23	"	203
Howe Uriah	Swanzey	"	P	"	23	"	205
Howe Benjamin	"	"	P	"	23	"	203
Humphrey Willard	"	"	P	"	23	"	205
Hutchins Asa – 2	Winchester	"	P	"	23	"	203
Hadley Stephen	Hudson	"	P	Ford's	20	"	206
Harris Thomas	Nashua	"	P	"	20	"	207
Harwood James	Litchfield	"	P	"	20	"	207
Haskell Abel	Merrimack	"	P	"	20	"	207
Honey Peter – 3	Nashua	"	P	"	20	"	207
Hutchinson Solomon – 4	Merrimack	"	P	"	20	"	207
Hardy Thomas – 5	Hollis	"	P	Goss's	20	"	209
Hartshorn Jonathan	Wilton	"	P	"	20	"	211
Herrick Shadrach	Mason	"	P	"	20	"	211
Hodgman Nathan	"	"	P	"	20	"	211
Hodgman Joseph Jr – 6	"	"	P	"	20	"	211
Hodgman Job	"	"	P	"	20	"	211
Hobart Joshua	Hollis	"	P	"	20	"	209
How Ephraim – 7	"	"	P	"	20	"	209
Harris Samuel	Amherst	"	P	Bradford's	19	"	214

1 — Wounded.

Gale John, Garland Jacob, Webster's Co., 'of Salisbury, — enlisted August 25, 1777. Vol. 15, 165.

1, 2, 3, 4, 5, 6, 7 — At Bunker Hill.

Name.	Residence.	Regiment.	Rank.	Company.	Enlisted.	Vol.	Page.
Hazelton Nathaniel	Amherst	Nichols's	Sergt	Bradford's	July 19	15	213
Hogg William	"	"	P	"	19	"	215
Holt Obadiah	"	"	P	"	19	"	214
Holt Daniel	Wilton	"	P	"	19	"	214
Howe Joel – 1	Amherst	"	Sergt	"	19	"	213
Hale Moses Jr	Rindge	"	P	Stone's	21	"	217
Harrington John	Fitzwilliam	"	Drum	"	21	"	216
Hathorn Collin	Jaffrey	"	P	"	21	"	217
Holt Thomas	"	"	P	"	21	"	217
Heald Joseph	Temple	"	P	Parker's	19	"	221
Hildreth Simeon – 2	New Ipswich	"	Fifer	"	19	"	219
Hogg Simpson	Peterborough	"	P	"	19	"	221
Hoar Jotham	New Ipswich	"	P	"	19	"	220
Haselton William – 3	Westmoreland	"	P	Carleton's	22	"	224
Haselton Richard	"	"	P	"	22	"	224
Hastings Josiah – 4	Chesterfield	"	Ensign	"	22	"	223
Hildreth Jonathan Jr	"	"	P	"	22	"	224
Holton Jonathan – 5	Westmoreland	"	Lieut	"	22	"	223
Hubbard Amos	Chesterfield	"	P	"	22	"	224
Hall Samuel	Keene	"	P	Mack's	22	"	227
Harris David – 6	"	"	P	"	22	"	227
Hayward Nathan – 7	Marlow	"	Corpl	"	22	"	226
Holbrook Adin	Keene	"	Sergt	"	22	"	226
Holdridge Jehial	Gilsum	"	Corpl	"	22	"	226
How Tilly – 8	Keene	"	Sergt	"	22	"	226
Hamblet Phinehas	Pelham	"	P	J Wilson's	21	"	229
Hardy Edmund	"	"	P	"	21	"	228
Hardy Jacob	Salem	"	P	"	21	"	228
Head James – 9	Pembroke	Stickney's	Major		23	"	161
Hall Josiah	Chester	"	P	Dearborn's	21	"	168
Hall David	"	"	P	"	21	"	170
Hazeltine Benjamin	"	"	P	"	21	"	169
Hills Samuel	"	"	P	"	21	"	168
Hoyt John	Warner	"	Sergt	Webster's	20	"	164
Huntoon Benjamin	Salisbury	"	P	"	20	"	164
Hackett Ezra	"	"	P	Taylor's	22	"	172
Hackett Hezekiah	"	"	P	"	22	"	173
Harper Samuel	Sanbornton	"	P	"	22	"	172
Hadley Obadiah	Dunbarton	"	P	McConnell's	19	"	176
Hadley Daniel	Weare	"	P	"	19	"	175
Harvey Enoch	Manchester	"	P	"	19	"	176
Hasket Ebenezer	"	"	P	"	19	"	177

1, 2, 4, 7, 8 — At Bunker Hill.
3, 5 — Wounded.
6 — At Bunker Hill; promoted August 20, 1777, to assistant surgeon. See original roll, Vol. 4, 17½.
9 — Wounded; died August 31, 1777.

Name.	Residence.	Regiment.	Rank.	Company.	Enlisted.	Vol.	Page.
Hawes Nathan	Goffstown	Stickney's	P	McConnell's	July 19	15	175
Hoit Samuel	"	"	P	"	19	"	175
Holden Zachariah	Litchfield	"	P	"	19	"	176
Holmes William Jr	Dunbarton	"	P	"	19	"	176
Holt Frye	Pembroke	"	P	"	19	"	175
Houston Samuel	Bedford	"	Corpl	"	19	"	174
Houston Isaac	"	"	P	"	19	"	175
Hoyt Thomas	Dunbarton	"	Ensign	"	19	"	174
Huntington John	Weare	"	P	"	19	"	177
Hannaford Peter	Canterbury	"	P	Sias's	20	"	179
Hancock Joseph	"	"	P	"	20	"	180
Hoyt Abner	"	"	P	"	20	"	180
Hadley Ezekiel	Hopkinton	"	Drum	Bayley's	21	"	182
Harriman Stephen Jr	"	"	P	"	22	"	183
Heath William	Henniker	"	P	"	22	"	183
Heath Sargent	"	"	P	"	22	"	183
Holmes Benjamin	Hopkinton	"	P	"	22	"	182
Howe Peter – [1]	"	"	Sergt	"	21	"	182
Howe David	"	"	P	"	21	"	182
Howe Samuel	"	"	P	"	21	"	182
Hunt Jonathan	"	"	P	"	21	"	183
Hall Abiel	Concord	"	P	Kimball's	20	"	186
Herbert Richard	"	"	Lieut	"	20	"	185
Hinkson Samuel	"	"	P	"	20	"	186
Hoit Jedediah	Boscawen	"	P	"	20	"	186
Hutchins John	"	"	P	"	20	"	186
Herrick Daniel	Lyndeborough	"	P	Clark's	21	"	189
Herrick Edmund	"	"	P	"	21	"	189
Holt William	"	"	P	"	21	"	189
Hooper Thomas – [2]	New Boston	"	P	"	21	"	189
Hogg William	Deering	"	P	"	21	"	189
Hutchinson Nehemiah – [3]	Lyndeborough	"	Sergt	"	21	"	188
Hutchinson Samuel – [4]	"	"	P	"	21	"	189
Haines Joseph	Wakefield	"	Corpl	Gilman's	20	"	191
Hanson Nathan	Middleton	"	P	"	20	"	192
Hicks John	"	"	P	"	20	"	192
Hill William	"	"	Corpl	"	20	"	191
Hill Ebenezer	"	"	P	"	20	"	191
Hutchinson Elisha – [5]	Gilmanton	"	Sergt	N Wilson's	22	"	194
Hobart David	Plymouth	Hobart's	Col		21	"	142
Heyward William	Charlestown	"	Major		25	"	142
Hibbard Augustine	Claremont	"	Chapl'n		Aug 4	"	142
Hart Josiah	Charlestown	"	P	Walker's	July 21	"	143
Hart John	"	"	P	"	21	"	145

1, 3, 4, 5 — At Bunker Hill.
2 — Wounded; died August 25, 1777.

Name.	Residence.	Regiment.	Rank.	Company.	Enlisted.	Vol.	Page.
Hastings Oliver	Charlestown	Hobart's	P	Walker's	July 21	15	143
Hatch Josiah	Claremont	"	P	"	21	"	145
Higbee Levi	"	"	P	"	21	"	144
Holden Timothy	Charlestown	"	P	"	21	"	143
Howard Benjamin – 1	Sunapee	"	P	"	21	"	144
Huntoon Caleb	Unity	"	Sergt	"	21	"	143
Huntoon Charles	"	"	P	"	21	"	144
Hall Abraham		"	P	Webber's	21	"	146
Hatch Nathan	Alstead	"	P	"	21	"	147
Hatch Asa	"	"	P	"	21	"	147
Hobart John		"	P	"	21	"	147
Hodgkins Henry		"	P	"	21	"	146
Howard David	Marlow	"	Corpl	"	21	"	146
Huntley Andrew	"	"	P	"	21	"	147
Hurd Stephen	Newport	"	P	"	21	"	147
Hall Henry	Rumney	"	Lieut	Elliot's	21	"	149
Hobart Solomon – 2	Plymouth	"	P	"	21	"	150
Hobart Gersham	"	"	P	"	21	"	150
Hoit Thomas – 3	Alexandria	"	P	"	21	"	150
Hazelton Timothy	Haverhill	. "	P	Post's	24	"	153
Hews Joseph	Lyme	"	P	"	24	"	153
Howard Benjamin	"	"	P	"	24	"	153
Hall Samuel R	Croydon	"	P	Hendee's	23	"	156
Hall Edward Jr	"	"	P	"	23	"	156
Harris Benjamin	Lebanon	"	P	"	23	"	156
Hendee Joshua	Hanover	"	Capt	"	23	"	155
Hilliard Samuel	Cornish	"	Drum	"	23	"	155
Howard Thomas	Grafton	"	P	"	23	"	157
Ingalls Henry – 4	Richmond	Nichols's	Lieut	Wright's	23	"	203
Ingalls Benjamin	"	"	P	"	23	"	204
Ingalls Joseph	"	"	P	"	23	"	204
Ingalls Ebenezer – 5	Jaffrey	"	P	Stone's	21	"	217
Ingalls Amos	Rindge	"	P	"	21	"	217
Ingalls Caleb	"	"	P	"	21	"	218
Ingalls Jonathan	Hill	Hobart's	P	Elliot's	21	"	150
Jones Jesse	Londonderry	Nichols's	P	Reynolds's	20	"	201
Johnson Joseph	Hudson	"	P	Ford's	20	"	206
Jewett Joseph	Amherst	"	P	Bradford's	19	"	215
Jones Caleb	"	"	P	"	19	"	213
Jewett Jonathan		"	P	Stone's	21	"	217
Jameson John	Windham	"	P	J Wilson's	21	"	228
Johnson Amos	Pelham	"	P	"	21	"	228
Jewell John	Sandwich	Stickney's	P	Taylor's	22	"	172

1, 3, 5 — At Bunker Hill.
2 — Killed.
4 — Wounded.
Hidden Jeremiah, Kimball's Co., enlisted August 24, 1777. Vol. 15, 187.

Name.	Residence.	Regiment.	Rank.	Company.	Enlisted.	Vol.	Page.
Judkins Ebenezer	Meredith	Stickney's	P	Taylor's	July 22	15	173
Johnson Benjamin	Canterbury	"	Corpl	Sias's	20	"	179
Jones Moses – [1]	Hopkinton	"	P	Bayley's	22	"	183
Jackman William	Boscawen	"	P	Kimball's	20	"	187
Johnson Timothy – [2]	Concord	"	P	"	20	"	186
Johnson Gideon	Middleton	"	Sergt	Gilman's	20	"	191
Jacobs Andrew	Barnstead	"	Corpl	N Wilson's	22	"	194
Jacobs David	"	"	P	"	22	"	195
Johnston Charles	Haverhill	Hobart's	Lieut Colonel		22	"	142
Johnson Job	Charlestown	"	P	Walker's	21	"	143
Joy Ephraim	Plainfield	"	P	Hendee's	23	"	155
Kelso Jonathan	Londonderry	Nichols's	P	Reynolds's	20	"	200
Kingsley Jonathan	Richmond	"	P	Wright's	23	"	204
Keith Jeremiah	Nashua	"	P	Ford's	20	"	207
Killicut Charity	"	"	P	"	20	"	207
Kemp Thomas – [3]	Hollis	"	P	Goss's	20	"	210
Kenney David	Wilton	"	P	"	20	"	211
Keys Silas	"	"	P	"	20	"	211
Kimball William	"	"	P	"	20	"	211
Kimball Eli	Amherst	"	P	Bradford's	19	"	213
Kittridge Solomon	"	"	P	"	19	"	214
Knowlton John	Dublin	"	Corpl	Stone's	21	"	216
Knight John	New Ipswich	"	P	Parker's	19	"	220
Keys Daniel	Westmoreland	"	P	Carleton's	22	"	225
Kyle Ephraim – [4]	Windham	"	Corpl	J Wilson's	21	"	228
Karr Thomas	"	"	P	"	21	"	229
Kincaid John – [5]	"	"	P	"	21	"	228
Kimball Amos	Chester	Stickney's	P	Dearborn's	21	"	169
Knowles John – [6]	"	"	P.	"	21	"	169
Knowles Amos – [7]	Candia	"	P	"	21	"	169
Kezar Reuben	Salisbury	"	P	Webster's	20	"	165
Kelly Samuel	Pembroke	"	P	McConnell's	19	"	176
Knox James	"	"	Corpl	"	19	"	174
Kenniston David	Canterbury	"	P	Sias's	20	"	180
Kimball Abraham – [8]	Hopkinton	"	P	Bayley's	22	"	183
Kimball Peter – [9]	Boscawen	"	Capt	Kimball's	20	"	185
Kenniston Waldron	Middleton	"	P	Gilman's	20	"	192
Kenniston Solomon	Gilmanton	"	P	N Wilson's	22	"	194

1, 3, 4, 7 — At Bunker Hill.
2 — Taken sick at Bennington ; sent to Charlestown and died there. Vol 11, 407.
5 — At Bunker Hill; killed at Bennington.
6, 9 — Wounded.
8 — At Bunker Hill; wounded at Bennington.
 Johnson James, Webster's Co., enlisted August 25, 1777. Vol. 15, 166.
 Jackson Stephen, Taylor's Co., discharged August 13. Vol. 15, 172.
 Jackman John, Kimball's Co., enlisted August 24, 1777. Vol. 15, 187.
 Johnson Robert, Post's Co., enlisted September 1, 1777. Vol. 15, 153.

Name.	Residence.	Regiment.	Rank.	Company.	Enlisted.	Vol.	Page.
Kimball Nathaniel	Gilmanton	Stickney's	P	N Wilson's	July 22	15	194
Kidder Stephen	Claremont	Hobart's	P	Walker's	21	"	144
Kelcey Seymore – [1]	Newport	"	P	Webber's	21	"	147
Kentfield George	Plymouth	"	Sergt	Elliot's	21	"	149
Keyes Ezekiel	"	"	Corpl	"	21	"	149
Kidder John	Hill	"	P	"	21	"	150
Ketcham Jonas	Hanover	"	P	Hendee's	23	"	157
Latham Arthur	Winchester	Nichols's	Corpl	Wright's	23	"	203
Lovewell Jonathan	Nashua	"	Sergt	Ford's	20	"	206
Lund Noah	"	"	P	"	20	"	207
Lovejoy Henry – [2]	Wilton	"	P	Goss's	20	"	211
Lakin Simeon	Hancock	"	P	Bradford's	19	"	214
Lampson Jonathan	Amherst	"	P	"	19	"	214
Lewis Asa – [3]	Milford	"	P	"	19	"	215
Lake Henry	Rindge	"	P	Stone's	21	"	217
Lewis Samuel	Peterborough	"	Corpl	Parker's	19	"	219
Little Thomas	"	"	P	"	19	"	221
Lowell Samuel – [4]	Washington	"	Drum	"	19	"	219
Leach Josiah Jr	Westmoreland	"	P	Carleton's	22	"	224
Lane Ezekiel – [5]	Raymond	Stickney's	Lieut	Dearborn's	19	"	167
Lane John Jr	Chester	"	Lieut	"	21	"	167
Leavitt Moses	Raymond	"	P	"	21	"	168
Libbey James	"	"	P	"	21	"	169
Loverin Samuel	Salisbury	"	Corpl	Webster's	20	"	164
Leach Billy	Moultonborough	"	P	Taylor's	22	"	172
Lougee John	Loudon	"	P	Sias's	20	"	180
Little Benjamin	Boscawen	"	P	Kimball's	20	"	186
Little Friend	"	"	P	"	20	"	186
Laiken Lemuel	Hancock	"	P	Clark's	21	"	188
Lewis Asa	Francestown	"	P	"	21	"	189
Lund Jesse – [6]	Lyndeborough	"	P	"	21	"	188
Lang Gilbert	"	"	P	Gilman's	20	"	192
Leavitt Carr	Effingham	"	Ensign	"	20	"	191
Leavitt Joseph	Wakefield	"	P	"	20	"	192
Lucas James	Wolfeborough	"	Sergt	"	20	"	191
Ladd Samuel	Gilmanton	"	Lieut	N Wilson's	22	"	194
Lougee Jesse	"	"	P	"	22	"	195
Lane Thomas	Newport	Hobart's	P	Webber's	21	"	147
Lowell Joseph	"	"	P	Elliot's	21	"	150
Ladd James	Haverhill	"	Drum	Post's	24	"	152
Ladd John	"	"	P	"	24	"	152
Lock William	"	"	P	"	24	"	153
Lock Elisha	"	"	P	"	24	"	153

1, 2, 4, 6 — At Bunker Hill.
3 — At Bunker Hill; killed at Bennington.
5 — Killed.
Ladd Josiah, Taylor's Co., discharged August 13, 1777. Vol. 15, 172.

Name.	Residence.	Regiment.	Rank.	Company.	Enlisted.	Vol.	Page.
Lurvey Peter	Piermont	Hobart's	P	Post's	July 24	15	153
McClary David – 1	Londonderry	Nichols's	Lieut	Reynolds's	20	"	199
McClary Thomas	"	"	P	"	20	"	201
McClary John	"	"	P	"	20	"	201
McDuffee Mansfield	Chester	"	P	"	20	"	200
McKeen John	Londonderry	"	Sergt	"	20	"	199
Moore James	"	"	P	"	20	"	200
Morrison Robert	"	"	P	"	20	"	200
Morrison James – 2	"	"	P	"	20	"	201
Marsh Jonathan	Hudson	"	P	Ford's	20	"	206
McClure David	"	"	Sergt	"	20	"	206
McClure Thomas – 3	Merrimack	"	P	"	20	"	207
McClure John	"	"	P	"	20	"	207
McQuig David – 4	Litchfield	"	Ensign	"	20	"	206
Merrill John	Hudson	"	Sergt	"	20	"	206
McDaniels James	Hollis	"	P	Goss's	20	"	210
McIntosh Archibald	Brookline	"	P	"	20	"	210
Merrill Samuel	Hollis	"	P	"	20	"	210
Messer Benjamin	"	"	P	"	20	"	210
Mooar Jacob	"	"	P	"	20	"	210
Mooar Daniel Jr	"	"	P	"	20	"	210
Morgan Ashley	Wilton	"	P	"	20	"	211
McClench Joseph	Amherst	"	Corpl	Bradford's	19	"	213
Merrill Benjamin	"	"	P	"	19	"	214
Mills John – 5	"	"	Lieut	"	19	"	213
Mason Benjamin	Dublin	"	Fifer	Stone's	21	"	216
Mason Moses	"	"	P	"	21	"	217
Mason Joseph	Nelson	"	P	"	21	"	217
McAllister Isaac	Marlborough	"	Sergt	"	21	"	216
Mixer Nathan – 6	Fitzwilliam	"	Sergt	"	21	"	216
Morse Reuben	Dublin	"	Ensign	"	21	"	216
Morse Jonathan	"	"	P	"	21	"	217
Morse Micah	"	"	P	"	21	"	217
McCoy Charles	Peterborough	"	P	Parker's	19	"	221
Miller Samuel	" .	"	P	"	19	"	221
Mitchell Benjamin	"	"	P	"	19	"	221
Mitchell James – 7	"	"	P	"	19	"	221
Mitchell Samuel – 8	"	"	Sergt	"	19	"	219
Moore William	"	"	P	"	19	"	221
Morrison Thomas – 9	"	"	Corpl	"	19	"	219
Metcalf Thomas	Chesterfield	"	P	Carleton's	22	"	223
Metcalf Joseph – 10	"	"	P	"	22	"	223
Mack Elisha	Gilsum	"	Capt	Mack's	22	"	226
Metcalf Michael – 11	Keene	"	P	"	22	"	227
Metcalf Ezra – 12	"	•	"	P	"	22	"	227

1, 2, 3, 4, 5, 7, 8, 9, 10, 12 — At Bunker Hill.
6, 11 — Killed at Bennington.

6

Name.	Residence.	Regiment.	Rank.	Company.	Enlisted.	Vol.	Page.
Marsh James	Hudson	Nichols's	P	J Wilson's	July 21	15	228
Marshall Benjamin – 1	"	"	P	"	21	"	228
McGlaughlin James	Windham	"	P	"	21	"	228
Morrison Samuel	"	"	Sergt	"	21	"	228
Morrow Alexander	"	"	P	"	21	"	228
Morgan Jonathan – 2	Wilton	"	P	"	21	"	228
Maxfield Nathaniel	Candia	Stickney's	P	Dearborn's	21	"	168
McFarland James	Chester	"	P	"	21	"	168
Morse Philip	Candia	"	P	"	21	"	169
Moore John – 3	"	"	P	"	21	"	170
Moore Samuel	"	"	P	"	21	"	169
Marston Paul S	Andover	"	Corpl	Webster's	20	"	164
McNeil John – 4	Hillsborough	"	P	"	20	"	165
Mitchel Philip	Andover	"	P	"	20	"	164
Morey William	"	"	P	"	20	"	165
Morse Joseph	Salisbury	"	Corpl	"	20	"	164
Marstin Jeremiah	Meredith	"	P	Taylor's	22	"	173
McGoon Alexander	Moultonborough	"	P	"	22	"	172
Morrison Jonathan	Meredith	"	P	"	22	"	173
Mudgett Thomas	"	"	P	"	22	"	172
Matthews Robert	Bedford	"	P	McConnell's	19	"	175
McAffee Samuel – 5	"	"	P	"	19	"	175
McClure David	Goffstown	"	P	"	19	"	175
McClure David Jr	"	"	P	"	19	"	174
McConnell Samuel	Pembroke	"	Capt	"	18	"	174
McCoy Charles – 6	Allenstown	"	P	"	19	"	175
McCurdy Archibald	Dunbarton	"	P	"	19	"	176
McLaughlin William	Bedford	"	P	"	19	"	175
McQuaid Jacob	"	"	P	"	19	"	176
Mills Thomas Jr	Dunbarton	"	P	"	19	"	176
Moore John	Bedford	"	P	"	19	"	175
Moore William	"	"	P	"	19	"	175
Morse Stephen	Pembroke	"	P	"	19	"	175
Morrison John	Bedford	"	P	"	19	"	176
Morrison David	"	"	P	"	19	"	176
Magoon Ephraim	Loudon	"	P	Sias's	20	"	180
Manuel Peter	Bow	"	P	"	20	"	180
Manuel Samuel	"	"	P	"	20	"	180
Marstin Benjamin	Loudon	"	P	"	20	"	180
Moore William	Canterbury	"	P	"	20	"	180
Morrill Laban	"	"	Lieut	"	20	"	179
Morrill Abraham	"	"	P	"	20	"	181
Morrill Isaac	Loudon	"	P	"	20	"	179
Moody Elisha	Concord	"	P	Bayley's	22	"	183

1, 2, 4, 6 -- At Bunker Hill.
3 — Wounded ; died August 21.
5 — Wounded ; died August 18.

Name.	Residence.	Regiment.	Rank.	Company.	Enlisted.	Vol.	Page.
Morse Samuel	Boscawen	Stickney's	P	Kimball's	July 20	15	186
Martin Samuel – [1]	Francestown	"	Corpl	Clark's	21	"	188
McAllister John	New Boston	"	P	"	21	"	188
McNeill Daniel	" "	"	P	"	21	"	189
Mellen Thomas – [2]	Francestown	"	P	"	21	"	189
Miltimore Daniel – [3]	Antrim	"	Lieut	"	21	"	188
Miller Thomas	Hancock	"	P	"	21	"	189
Mills Joseph	Deering	"	P	"	21	"	189
Mills Joseph	"	"	Sergt	Gilman's	20	"	191
McCluer James	Acworth	Hobart's	Lieut	Walker's	21	"	143
McRoberts John	Springfield	"	P	"	21	"	143
Mack Silas	Marlow	"	Corpl	Webber's	21	"	146
Mack Joseph Jr	Alstead	"	P	"	21	"	147
Marcy John Jr	Walpole	"	P	"	21	"	147
Merriam John Jr	"	"	P	"	21	"	146
Marsh Samuel	Plymouth	"	Corpl	Elliot's	21	"	149
McMurphy Daniel – [4]	Alexandria	"	Lieut	"	21	"	149
McConnell Thomas	Lyman	"	Sergt	Post's	24	"	152
Merrill John	Bath	"	P	"	24	"	153
Morey Ephraim	Orford	"	Sergt	"	24	"	152
Mason Russell	Grafton	"	Sergt	Hendee's	23	"	155
Mason Nathaniel	"	"	P	"	23	"	157
Mason Robert	Hanover	"	P	"	23	"	157
Nichols Moses	Amherst	Nichols's	Col		18	"	198
Nesmith James – [5]	Londonderry	"	P	Reynolds's	20	"	200
Nichols Andrew	Swanzey	"	P	Wright's	23	"	203
Nichols Jonathan Jr	"	"	P	"	23	"	204
Nevins Benjamin	Hollis	"	P	Goss's	20	"	210
Nevins John	"	"	P	"	20	"	210
Nichols Aaron		"	P	Bradford's	19	"	213
Newell Jacob	Marlborough	"	P	Stone's	21	"	218
Noyce John		"	P	Mack's	22	"	227
Nickerson Reuben	Moultonborough	Stickney's	P	Taylor's	22	"	173
Norris Joseph	Pembroke	"	P	McConnell's	19	"	175
Nutt John	Manchester	"	P	"	19	"	176
Norris David	Canterbury	"	P	Sias's	20	"	179
Nichols John	Francestown	"	P	Clark's	21	"	189
Nutter Grafton		"	P	Gilman's	20	"	192
Nelson Joseph	Barnstead	"	P	N Wilson's	22	"	195
Nichols Timothy	Lempster	Hobart's	Sergt	Webber's	21	"	146
Olcott Benjamin	Swanzey	Nichols's	P	Wright's	23	"	203
Odell Ebenezer	Amherst	"	P	Bradford's	19	"	215

1, 5 — At Bunker Hill.
2 –– Living in 1848, aged 92.
3 –– At Bunker Hill; formerly of Londonderry.
4 — Wounded.
    Newton William, Webster's Co., enlisted August 25, 1777. Vol. 15, 165.

Name.	Residence.	Regiment.	Rank.	Company.	Enlisted.	Vol.	Page.
Osgood Enoch	Raymond	Stickney's	P	Dearborn's	July 21	15	168
Orr John – [1]	Bedford	"	Lieut	McConnell's	19	"	174
Osgood William	Claremont	Hobart's	P	Walker's	21	"	144
Peabody Stephen – [2]	Amherst		Major		18	"	141
Page Eli	Richmond	Nichols's	P	Wright's	23	"	204
Parker Reuben	"	"	P	"	23	"	205
Parker Robert	Litchfield	"	P	Ford's	20	"	207
Patterson Peter	"	"	P	"	20	"	207
Pemberton James – [3]	Hudson	"	Corpl	"	20	"	206
Pollard Thomas	"	"	P	"	20	"	207
Parkhurst Jesse	Wilton	"	P	Goss's	20	"	211
Pierce Asa – [4]	"	"	P	"	20	"	211
Peirce Ephraim – [5]	Hollis	"	P	"	20	"	210
Powers Samson – [6]	"	"	P	"	20	"	210
Powers Francis – [7]	"	"	P	"	20	"	210
Parker William – [8]	Wilton	"	P	Bradford's	19	"	213
Patterson John	Amherst	"	Ensign	"	19	"	213
Pettingill Joshua – [9]	"	"	P	"	19	"	215
Pettingill Moses	"	"	P	"	19	"	214
Page Reuben – [10]	Rindge	"	P	Stone's	21	"	217
Perry Ebenezer – [11]	Wilton	"	Lieut	"	21	"	216
Perkins Elisha	Rindge	"	P	"	21	"	217
Platts Joseph Jr	"	"	P	"	21	"	217
Potter Ebenezer	Fitzwilliam	"	Corpl	"	21	"	216
Proctor Isaac	Jaffrey	"	P	"	21	"	217
Pratt Asa	Dublin	"	P	"	21	"	217
Parker Stephen	New Ipswich	"	Capt	Parker's	19	"	219
Parker Jonathan	"	"	P	"	19	"	220
Paige Sargent	Peterborough	"	P	"	19	"	221
Powers Whitcomb	New Ipswich	"	Corpl	"	19	"	219
Powers Paul	Temple	"	P	"	19	"	220
Proctor Jeremiah – [12]	Stoddard	"	P	"	19	"	221
Partridge Amos	Chesterfield	"	P	Carleton's	22	"	224
Peacock Samuel	"	"	P	"	22	"	225
Peacock James	Hinsdale	"	P	"	22	"	224
Pierce Amos	Westmoreland	"	Lieut	"	22	"	223
Pierce Benjamin	"	"	P	"	22	"	224
Packard Gideon		"	P	Mack's	22	"	226
Puffer Amos	Keene	"	P	"	22	"	227
Peterson Daniel	Boscawen	Stickney's	Assistant Surgeon		23	"	161
Pattin David	Chester	"	P	Dearborn's	21	"	169
Pattin John	"	"	P	"	21	"	168
Peavey Joseph		"	P	"	21	"	167

1 — Wounded.
2, 3, 4, 5, 6, 7, 8, 9, 10 — At Bunker Hill.
11 — Killed.
12 — At Bunker Hill; wounded; died August 23, 1777.

Name.	Residence.	Regiment.	Rank.	Company.	Enlisted.	Vol.	Page.
Perkins Benjamin		Stickney's	P	Dearborn's	July 21	15	169
Perkins David	"	"	P	"	21	"	168
Pillsbury Joseph	Candia	"	P	"	21	"	169
Presbury James	Chester	"	P	"	21	"	168
Prescott William P	Raymond	"	P	"	21	"	169
Palmer John – 1	Warner	"	P	Webster's	20	"	165
Palmer Simeon	"	"	P	"	20	"	165
Pope William	Hillsborough	"	Ensign	"	20	"	164
Preston Samuel	"	"	P	"	20	"	165
Pressey Paskey	Warner	"	Sergt	"	20	"	164
Purmot Richard	Salisbury	"	P	"	20	"	164
Plaisted Samuel	New Hampton	"	P	Taylor's	22	"	172
Poland Josiah	Ossipee	"	P	"	22	"	172
Page Caleb Jr	Dunbarton	"	P	McConnell's	19	"	176
Piper Samuel – 2	Pembroke	"	P	"	19	"	175
Perkins William	Canterbury	"	Drum	Sias's	20	"	179
Parsons Noah – 3	Hopkinton	"	Corpl	Bayley's	22	"	182
Patterson Isaac	Henniker	"	P	"	22	"	183
Pope Thomas	"	"	P	"	22	"	183
Powell Moses	"	"	P	"	22	"	183
Putney Asa – 4	"	"	Sergt	"	22	"	182
Putney John – 5	"	"	P	"	22	"	183
Pearson Isaac	Boscawen	"	P	Kimball's	20	"	186
Pettingill Andrew – 6	Salisbury	"	Ensign	"	20	"	185
Peters John	Concord	"	P	"	20	"	186
Potter Anthony	"	"	P	"	20	"	187
Parsons George	Lyndeborough	"	Corpl	Clark's	21	"	188
Patterson William	New Boston	"	P	"	21	"	189
Pringle Thomas	Greenfield	"	P	"	21	"	189
Page John		"	P	Gilman's	20	"	192
Perkins Benjamin	Wakefield	"	Drum	"	20	"	191
Perkins Joseph	"	"	Fifer	"	20	"	191
Phelps)Davenport	Orford	Hobart's	Q M		25	"	142
Porter Noah	Charlestown	"	P	Walker's	21	"	144
Powers Joseph – 7	"	"	Sergt	"	21	"	143
Powers Asahel	Claremont	"	P	"	21	"	144
Powers Whitcomb	Charlestown	"	P	"	21	"	145
Putnam Thomas	Acworth	"	P	"	21	"	144
Paul James		"	Corpl	Webber's	21	"	146
Palmer Jonathan	Alexandria	"	P	Elliot's	21	"	150
Patterson George	Plymouth	"	P	"	21	"	149
Powers William	"	"	P	"	21	"	150
Palmer Amos	Orford	"	P	Post's	24	"	153
Parker Samuel	Lyman	"	P	"	24	"	153

1, 2, 3, 5, 7 — At Bunker Hill.
4 — Wounded.
6 — Wounded ; died December 12, 1777.

7

Name.	Residence.	Regiment.	Rank.	Company.	Enlisted.	Vol.	Page.
Patterson Ephraim	Piermont	Hobart's	Ensign	Post's	July 24	15	152
Porter Thomas	Lyme	"	P	"	24	"	153
Post Jeremiah – [1]	Orford	"	Capt	"	24	"	152
Post Eldad	"	"	P	"	. 24	"	153
Prentice Benjamin	Lyman	"	P	"	24	"	153
Parker Ezekiel	Hanover	"	P	Hendee's	23	"	157
Peck Walter	Lebanon	"	P	"	23	"	156
Porter Eleazer M	"	"	P	"	23	"	156
Quimby Caleb	Meredith	Stickney's	P	Taylor's	22	"	173
Quimby Isaac	Hopkinton	"	P	Bayley's	22	"	183
Ramsey William	Londonderry	Nichols's	P	Reynolds's	20	"	200
Reynolds Daniel	"	"	Capt	"	20	"	199
Robinson John – [2]	"	"	Sergt	"	20	"	199
Robinson John	"	"	P	"	20	"	199
Robinson Peter	"	"	P	"	20	"	200
Rogers Thomas	"	"	P	"	20	"	201
Rowell Samuel – [3]	"	"	P	"	20	"	200
Razey Peletiah	Richmond	"	P	Wright's	23	"	205
Roby Thomas	Nashua	"	P	Ford's	20	"	207
Robie Benjamin	"	"	P	"	20	"	207
Robbins Peter	Nashua	"	P	"	20	"	207
Rolfe Ephraim – [4]	Hollis	"	P	Goss's	20	"	210
Runnels Stephen	"	"	P	"	20	"	210
Russ Jonathan	"	"	Corpl	"	20	"	209
Russell Andrew	Brookline	"	P	"	20	"	210
Russell Pomp	Wilton	"	P	"	20	"	211
Ray James	Amherst	"	P	Bradford's	19	"	215
Robinson David	Rindge	"	P	Stone's	21	"	218
Ross Abraham	Jaffrey	"	P	"	21	"	217
Russell Reuben	Rindge	"	P	"	21	"	217
Robb John – [5]	Stoddard	"	Sergt	Parker's	19	"	219
Robb William	Peterborough	"	P	"	19	"	221
Rumrill David	New Ipswich	"	P	"	19	"	219
Ranstead John – [6]	Westmoreland	"	P	Carleton's	22	"	225
Read John	Chesterfield	"	P	"	22	"	223
Robbins Samuel – [7]	Westmoreland	"	Corpl	"	22	"	223
Robbins Jonathan	"	"	P	"	22	"	224
Robbins Solomon	"	"	P	"	22	"	224
Robbins John	"	"	P	"	22	"	225
Robbins Eleazer – [8]	"	"	P	"	22	"	224

1 — Wounded ; died August 26, 1777.
2, 3, 4, 7, 8 — At Bunker Hill.
5 — Wounded.
6 — Killed.

Pettengill Matthew, Pettengill David, Webster's Co., enlisted August 25, 1777.   Vol. 15, 165.
Pearson Joseph, Boscawen, Kimball's Co., enlisted August 24, 1777.   Vol 15, 187.
Plumer Bitfield, Boscawen, Kimball's Co., enlisted August 24, 1777.   Vol. 15, 187.

Name.	Residence.	Regiment.	Rank.	Company.	Enlisted.	Vol.	Page.
Redding John	Surry	Nichols's	P	Mack's	July 22	15	227
Rhodes Timothy	"	"	P	"	22	"	227
Richardson Josiah	Keene	"	Lieut	"	22	"	226
Rowe John	Gilsum	"	Drum	"	22	"	226
Rollins Joseph	"	"	P	J Wilson's	21	"	228
Richardson Bradbury	Moultonborough	Stickney's	Major		23	"	161
Richardson James	Chester	"	P	Dearborn's	21	"	168
Robie Samuel	"	"	P	"	21	"	168
Robie Ichabod	Candia	"	P	"	21	"	168
Rollins Joseph	"	"	P	"	21	"	169
Rowe Robert	Chester	"	P	"	21	"	167
Robinson Joseph	Meredith	"	P	Taylor's	22	"	173
Rowe Reuben	Moultonborough	"	P	"	22	"	172
Remick Samuel – 1	Goffstown	"	P	McConnell's	19	"	175
Richards Eliphalet	."	"	P	"	19	"	174
Richards Amos	"	"	P	"	19	"	175
Riddle Hugh	Bedford	"	P	"	19	"	176
Roach Patrick		"	Fifer	"	19	"	174
Robinson John – 2	Pembroke	"	P	"	19	"	175
Rowell John		"	P	"	19	"	176
Rawlings Nathaniel	Loudon	"	P	Sias's	20	"	180
Rogers Joseph	Bow	"	Sergt	"	20	"	179
Rider Ebenezer	Hopkinton	"	P	Bayley's	22	"	183
Ross Lemuel	Henniker	"	P	"	22	"	183
Rowe Josiah	Hopkinton	"	P	"	22	"	183
Roberts Francis		"	P	Gilman's	20	"	191
Runnolds Abraham		"	P	"	20	"	192
Richardson Jeremiah	Gilmanton	"	P	N Wilson's	22	"	194
Roberts Joseph	Alton	"	P	"	22	"	195
Rundlet Charles	Gilmanton	"	P	"	22	"	195
Robbins Jonathan	Plymouth	Hobart's	Adjt		25	"	142
Remington Samuel	Charlestown	"	Corpl	Walker's	21	"	143
Rogers James	Acworth	"	Corpl	"	21	"	143
Royce Lemuel	Charlestown	"	P	"	21	"	143
Royce Silas	Claremont	"	P	"	21	"	144
Rumrill Simon	Alstead	"	P	Webber's	21	"	147
Richardson Obadiah	Plymouth	"	P	Elliot's	21	"	150
Rice Ebenezer	Haverhill	"	Lieut	Post's	24	"	152
Ripley William	Cornish	"	Sergt	Hendee's	23	"	155
Stark John – 3	Manchester		Gen		18	"	141
Smith Robert	Londonderry	Nichols's	Adjt		23	"	198
Sargent Joseph	"	"	P	Reynolds's	20	"	199
Senter Simeon	"	"	Corpl	"	20	"	199
Severance William – 4	"	"	P	"	20	"	200
Smith John – 5	"	"	Sergt	"	20	"	199

1 — Wounded.
2, 3, 4, 5 — At Bunker Hill.

Name.	Residence.	Regiment.	Rank.	Company.	Enlisted.	Vol.	Page.
Spear Samuel	Londonderry	Nichols's	P	Reynold's	July 20	15	200
Steel Joseph	"	"	P	"	20	"	201
Stevens Alexander	"	"	P	"	20	"	199
Stuart John	"	"	P	"	20	"	201
Switzer Nathaniel	Deering	"	P	"	20	"	200
Scott Samuel	Winchester	"	P	Wright's	23	"	205
Shafter James	Richmond	"	P	"	23	"	204
Starkey Peter	"	"	P	"	23	"	205
Stearns John	Winchester	"	Lieut	"	23	"	203
Severance Caleb	"	"	P	Ford's	20	"	206
Smith Samuel	Hudson	"	P	"	20	"	206
Snow Joseph	Nashua	"	P	"	20	"	207
Stewart Joel – [1]	"	"	Corpl	"	20	"	206
Sawyer Jonathan	"	"	P	Goss's	20	"	211
Shedd Jonas	Brookline	"	P	"	20	"	210
Shedd Daniel	Mason	"	P	"	20	"	211
Stearns Josiah	Hollis	"	P	"	20	"	210
Stearns Isaac – [2]	"	"	P	"	20	"	210
Stiles Joseph – [3]	Wilton	"	Sergt	"	20	"	209
Squires Samuel	Mason	"	P	"	20	"	211
Sawyer Benjamin	Amherst	"	P	Bradford's	19	"	214
Shannon Andrew	"	"	P	"	19	"	215
Stearns Benjamin – [4]	"	"	P	"	19	"	214
Stevens Caleb – [5]	"	"	P	"	19	"	214
Stewart Simpson	"	"	P	"	19	"	214
Stewart Samuel	"	"	P	"	19	"	214
Symonds Joseph	"	"	P	"	19	"	215
Sawtell Jonathan Jr	Rindge	"	P	Stone's	21	"	217
Sherwin David	"	"	P	"	21	"	217
Smith Henry	"	"	P	"	21	"	218
Smiley John	Jaffrey	"	P	"	21	"	217
Stanley John	"	"	Lieut	"	21	"	216
Stickney Simon	"	"	P	"	21	"	217
Stickney Lemuel	Jaffrey	"	P	"	21	"	217
Stone Salmon	Rindge	"	Capt	"	21	"	216
Stone Abel	"	"	Sergt	"	21	"	216
Stroud John – [6]	Nelson	"	P	"	21	"	217
Safford Benjamin	New Ipswich	"	P	Parker's	19	"	219
Sawtell Edmund	"	"	P	"	19	"	220
Severence Ebenezer – [7]	Temple	"	P	"	19	"	220
Severence Benjamin	"	"	P	"	19	"	220
Shattuck Nathaniel	"	"	P	"	19	"	220
Smith Jeremiah	Peterborough	"	P	"	19	"	221
Smith Jesse	Stoddard	"	P	"	19	"	221
Spaulding Levi	New Ipswich	"	P	"	19	"	220
Spaulding Henry	Stoddard	"	P	"	19	"	220

1, 2, 3, 4, 5, 6, 7 — At Bunker Hill.

Name	Residence.	Regiment.	Rank.	Company.	Enlisted.	Vol.	Page.
Stevens Ephraim [1]	New Ipswich	Nichols's	P	Parker's	July 19	15	220
Stewart John	Peterborough	"	P	"	19	"	221
Stickney Sile R	Temple	"	P	"	19	"	220
Stratton Nehemiah	New Ipswich	"	P	"	19	"	220
Sawyer Jonathan	Westmoreland	"	Sergt	Carleton's	22	"	223
Sawyer Ephraim	"	"	Sergt	"	22	"	223
Shattuck Daniel	Hinsdale	"	P	"	22	"	225
Snow Hosea	Westmoreland	"	P	"	22	"	224
Stoddard Lemuel	Chesterfield	"	P	"	22	"	223
Stone Jacob	Westmoreland	"	P	"	22	"	224
Streetor Benjamin	Chesterfield	"	P	"	22	"	224
Sawyer James	"	"	P	Mack's	22	"	227
Smith Jonathan	Surry	"	P	"	22	"	227
Stickney Thomas	Concord	Stickney's	Col		20	"	161
Smith Benjamin	Candia	"	P	Dearborn's	21	"	168
Smith Oliver	"	"	P	"	21	"	169
Swain Levi	Raymond	"	Corpl	"	21	"	167
Sanborn John	Salisbury	"	Drum	Webster's	20	"	164
Sawyer Edmund	Warner	"	P	"	20	"	165
Scribner Benjamin	Salisbury	"	P	"	20	"	165
Scribner Addo	"	"	P	"	20	"	165
Searle William	"	"	P	"	20	"	164
Severence Peter		"	P	"	20	"	165
Shephard Daniel	Boscawen	"	P	"	20	"	165
Sleeper Jedediah	Andover	"	P	"	20	"	164
Sleeper Thomas	"	"	P	"	20	"	165
Symonds William	Hillsborough	"	P	"	20	"	165
Sanborn Daniel T	Sanbornton	"	P	Taylor's	22	"	171
Sanborn Jonathan H	"	"	P	"	22	"	173
Scribner Nathaniel	Sandwich	"	P	"	22	"	172
Scribner Stephen	"	"	P	"	22	"	172
Sibley Samuel	Meredith	"	P	"	22	"	173
Sinkler Thomas	"	"	P	"	22	"	173
Sinkler Richard	Sandwich	"	P	"	22	"	172
Smart Robert	Sanbornton	"	P	"	22	"	171
Smith Timothy	"	"	P	"	22	"	173
Somes Timothy	Meredith	"	P	"	22	"	172
Swain Abraham	"	"	Sergt	"	22	"	171
Swain Ichabod	Sanbornton	"	P	"	22	"	171
Sargent Isaac	Weare	"	P	McConnell's	19	"	175
Sargent Enoch	Dunbarton	"	Corpl	"	19	"	174
Smith Adam	Bedford	"	P	"	19	"	175
Spear Robert	Goffstown	"	Corpl	"	19	"	174
Stevens Benjamin Jr	"	"	P	"	19	"	174
Stevens Benjamin 3ᵈ	"	"	P	"	19	"	175
Story Daniel	Dunbarton	"	P	"	19	"	176

1 — At Bunker Hill.

8

Name.	Residence.	Regiment.	Rank.	Company.	Enlisted.	Vol.	Page.
Sanborn Simon	Canterbury	Stickney's	P	Sias's	July 20	15	180
Sherburn James	Loudon	"	Corpl	"	20	"	179
Sias Benjamin	"	"	Capt	"	20	"	179
Sutton Stephen	Canterbury	"	P	"	20	"	180
Sargent Anthony	Hopkinton	"	P	Bayley's	22	"	183
Symonds Simeon	Henniker	"	Fifer	"	22	"	182
Smith Richard	Hopkinton	"	P	"	21	"	182
Smith Moses	Henniker	"	P	"	22	"	183
Stanley Joseph	Hopkinton	"	Q M	"	22	"	182
Stone Ezekiel	Henniker	"	P	"	22	"	183
Storey Thomas	Hopkinton	"	Sergt	"	21	"	182
Straw Jonathan Jr	"	"	P	"	22	"	183
Stevens Phinehas	Concord	"	P	Kimball's	20	"	187
Symms William – [1]	"	"	P	"	20	"	187
Smith John	New Boston	"	P	Clark's	21	"	189
Stiles John	Lyndeborough	"	P	"	21	"	189
Small Samuel		"	P	Gilman's	20	"	192
Smart Winthrop	Barnstead	"	Ensign	N Wilson's	22	"	194
Stevens Benjamin	Gilmanton	"	Corpl	"	22	"	194
Sweat Elisha	"	"	P	"	22	"	195
Silsby Eliphas	Acworth	Hobart's	P	Walker's	21	"	144
Simonds Levi	Charlestown	"	P	"	21	"	143
Simonds John	"	"	P	"	21	"	144
Sisco William	Sunapee	"	P	"	21	"	144
Spofford Asa	Charlestown	"	P	"	21	"	144
Spencer John	Claremont	"	P	"	21	"	145
Spooner James	"	"	P	"	21	"	145
Stevens Henry	"	"	P	"	21	"	145
Scovill Jesse	Marlow	"	P	Webber's	21	"	147
Simons William	Alstead	"	Sergt	"	21	"	146
Stearns Aaron	Walpole	"	Corpl	"	21	"	146
Stevens Josiah	Newport	"	Ensign	"	21	"	146
Stowell David Jr	"	"	Drum	"	21	"	146
Sargent Jacob	Thornton	"	P	Elliot's	21	"	149
Snow Nehemiah	Plymouth	"	P	"	21	"	150
Stearns Peter	"	"	P	"	21	"	150
Sanborn Richard	Haverhill	"	P	Post's	24	"	153
Sawyer Abel	Orford	"	Corpl	"	24	"	152
Shuff Jacob	Lisbon	"	Corpl	"	24	"	152
Stark Phinehas	Lyme	"	P	"	24	"	153
Smith Joseph	Plainfield	"	Lieut	Hendee's	23	"	155
Smith Lemuel	"	"	P	"	23	"	155
Taylor Adam	Londonderry	Nichols's	Lieut	Reynolds's	20	"	199
Taylor James	"	"	P	"	20	"	200
Taylor Samuel	"	"	P	"	20	"	201

1 — Wounded.
Smith Robert, Lieut., Smith John, Private, of Salisbury, Webster's Co.; enlisted August 25, 1777. Vol. 15, 164.

Name.	Residence.	Regiment.	Rank.	Company.	Enlisted.	Vol.	Page.
Thompson Samuel	Londonderry	Nichols's	P	Reynolds's	July 20	15	200
Todd Andrew	"	"	P	"	20	"	201
Todd John	"	"	P	"	20	"	201
Taylor Simeon	"	"	P	Wright's	23	"	205
Thayer Jonathan	Richmond	"	P	"	23	"	204
Tubbs Ananias – 1	Swanzey	"	P	"	23	"	203
Tarbell Thomas Jr	Mason	"	Corpl	Goss's	20	"	209
Tarbell Nathaniel	"	"	P	"	20	"	211
Townsend Ebenezer – 2	Hollis	"	P	"	20	"	210
Towne Thomas	Wilton	"	P	"	20	"	211
Taylor Benjamin	Amherst	"	P	Bradford's	19	"	214
Trevitt Henry	"	"	P	"	19	"	213
Tenny William	Marlborough	"	Corpl	Stone's	21	"	216
Tolman Benjamin – 3	Fitzwilliam	"	P	"	21	"	218
Tozer John	Marlborough	"	P	"	21	"	216
Taylor Abraham	Stoddard	"	P	Parker's	19	"	221
Taylor Silas – 4	"	"	P	"	19	"	221
Tisdale Benoni – 5	Westmoreland	"	Fifer	Carleton's	22	"	223
Tarbox John	Pelham	"	P	J Wilson's	21	"	228
Thomas Elisha		Stickney's	P	Dearborn's	21	"	169
Todd Daniel	Raymond	"	P	"	21	"	169
Towle William – 6	"	"	P	"	21	"	168
Towle Brackett	Chester	"	Sergt	"	21	"	167
Towle Simeon	"	"	P	"	21	"	168
Tilton Ebenezer	Andover	"	P	Webster's	20	"	165
Tucker Joseph	"	"	P	"	20	" .	165
Taylor Chase	Sanbornton	"	Capt	Taylor's	22	"	171
Taylor Jonathan Sen	"	"	Corpl	"	22	"	171
Thompson Jonathan	"	"	P	"	22	"	171
Thresher Joseph	Sandwich	"	P	"	22	"	172
Trussell Reuben – 7	Weare	"	P	McConnell's	19	"	177
Tyler Jeptha – 8	Pembroke	"	Sergt	"	19	"	174
Tebbetts Ephraim	Loudon •	"	Corpl	Sias's	20	"	179
Tebbetts Henry	"	"	P	"	20	"	180
Trumble Simon	Concord	"	P	Kimball's	20	"	187
Taplin John	Lyndeborough	"	P	Clark's	21	"	189
Tibbets Edmund	Wolfeborough	"	P	Gilman's	20	"	192
Towle John		"	Corpl	"	20	"	191
Tasker Paul	Barnstead	"	P	N Wilson's	22	"	195
Tibbetts Robert	"	"	P	"	22	"	194
Tucker John	Gilmanton	"	P	"	22	"	194
Taylor Joel	Plymouth	Hobart's	Sergt	Elliot's	21	"	149

1 — Wounded.
2, 3, 4, 6, 8 — At Bunker Hill.
5 — Killed.
7 — At Bunker Hill; wounded at Bennington.
    True Jacob, Webster's Co., enlisted August 25. Vol. 15, 165.

Name.	Residence.	Regiment.	Rank.	Company.	Enlisted.	Vol.	Page.
Taylor Jonathan	Alexandria	Hobart's	P	Elliot's	July 21	15	150
Taylor Medad	Hanover	"	P	Hendee's	23	"	157
Taylor Daniel	"	"	P	"	23	"	157
Tilden Joel	Lebanon	"	P	"	23	"	156
Tenney Reuben	Hanover	"	P	"	23	"	157
Usher Eleazer – [1]	Merrimack	Nichols's	P	Ford's	20	"	207
Upton William	Temple	"	P	Parker's	19	"	220
Underhill John	Chester	Stickney's	Corpl	Dearborn's	21	"	167
Underhill David	"	"	Corpl	"	21	"	167
Uran Daniel	Boscawen	"	P	Kimball's	20	"	187
Vickery John	Merrimack	Nichols's	P	Ford's	20	"	207
Verry John	Claremont	Hobart's	P	Walker's	21	"	145
Vaughan Jabez	Lyme	"	Lieut	Post's	24	"	152
Wallace Thomas	Londonderry	Nichols's	P	Reynolds's	20	"	200
Wallace Thomas Jr	"	"	P	"	20	"	201
Wallace Jonathan	"	"	P	"	20	"	201
Wallace John	"	"	P	"	20	"	201
Watts Hugh – [2]	"	"	P	"	20	"	201
Watts John	"	"	P	"	20	"	201
Wescott James	Richmond	"	P	Wright's	23	"	204
Whitcomb John	Swanzey	"	P	"	23	"	203
Wilson Samuel	"	"	P	"	23	"	205
Wood Jonathan	Winchester	"	Sergt	"	23	"	203
Woolley John	Richmond	"	P	"	23	"	204
Wright Samuel – [3]	Swanzey	"	Capt	"	23	"	203
Whittle Thomas	Litchfield	"	P	Ford's	20	"	207
Winn Joseph	Hudson	"	P	"	20	"	206
Wright Zebedee	Nashua	"	P	"	20	"	207
Wallingford David – [4]	Hollis	"	Lieut	Goss's	20	"	209
Weathee Daniel	Mason	"	P	"	20	"	211
Wheeler Abner	Hollis	"	P	"	20	"	210
Wood William – [5]	"	"	Sergt	"	20	"	209
Woods Jonas	"	"	P	"	20	"	210
Worcester Noah Jr – [6]	"	"	Fifer	"	20	"	209
Wright Benjamin	"	"	Corpl	"	20	"	209
Wright Samuel – [7]	"	"	P	"	20	"	210
Wyman Jesse	"	"	P	"	20	"	210
Wallace John	Amherst	"	P	Bradford's	19	"	213
Wilkins Jonathan – [8]	"	"	Sergt	"	19	"	213
Wilkins Eli	"	"	P	"	19	"	214
Wilson George	"	"	P	"	19	"	215
Webster Peter – [9]	Rindge	"	P	Stone's	21	"	217
Wilson Joseph – [10]	"	"	P	"	21	"	218
Winch Samuel	Fitzwilliam	"	P	"	21	"	218
Woodbury Luke	"	"	P	"	21	"	217

1, 2, 3, 4, 5, 6, 7, 8, 9 — At Bunker Hill.
10 — Killed.

Name.	Residence.	Regiment.	Rank.	Company.	Enlisted.	Vol.	Page.
Wright John	Dublin	Nichols's	P	Stone's	July 21	15	216
Walker Samuel	New Ipswich	"	P	Parker's	19	"	219
Walton Josiah Jr - 1	" "	"	P	"	19	"	219
Wheeler Richard	" "	"	P	"	19	"	220
Wheeler Amos	" "	"	P	"	19	"	220
Wheeler Samuel	Temple	"	P	"	19	"	220
Wheeler Peter	"	"	P	"	19	"	220
White Archibald - 2	Washington	"	Sergt	"	19	"	219
White James	Peterborough	"	P	"	19	"	221
Whittemore Zebediah	New Ipswich	"	P	"	19	"	219
Williams Benjamin - 3	" "	"	Ensign	"	19	"	219
Warner John	Westmoreland	"	P	Carleton's	22	"	224
Wheeler Josiah	Hinsdale	"	P	"	22	"	225
Willis Jonathan	Westmoreland	"	P	"	22	"	224
Winslow Luther - 4	Hinsdale	"	Corpl	"	22	"	223
Wheeler Jonathan - 5	Keene	"	P	Mack's	22	"	227
Wheeler Zadock	"	"	P	"	22	"	227
Wilcox Asa	Gilsum	"	Corpl	"	22	"	226
Wilson Daniel	Keene	"	P	"	22	"	227
Wilson David	"	"	P	"	22	"	227
Woods William - 6	"	"	P	"	22	"	227
Worsley Robert - 7	Marlborough	"	Corpl	"	22	"	226
Whiting Nathan - 8	Pelham	"	P	J Wilson's	21	"	229
Wilson Jesse	"	"	Capt	"	21	"	228
Wilson James	Windham	"	P	"	21	"	228
Wyman Jesse	Pelham	"	P	"	21	"	228
Wyman Levi	"	"	P	"	21	"	229
Wadleigh Benjamin	Candia	Stickney's	P	Dearborn's	21	"	169
Webster Moses - 9	Chester	"	P	"	21	"	169
Webster Moses Jr	"	"	P	"	21	"	168
West Wilks	"	"	P	"	21	"	169
White Joseph	"	"	P	"	21	"	168
Wilson Robert	"	"	Ensign	"	21	"	167
Wilson Robert Jr	Candia	"	P	"	21	"	169
Wilson Thomas - 10	"	"	P	"	21	"	169
Watkins Abner	Warner	"	P	Webster's	20	"	165
Webster Ebenezer	Salisbury	"	Capt	"	20	"	164
Webster Stephen	Sandwich	"	P	Taylor's	22	"	173
Winslow Samuel	"	"	Sergt	"	22	"	171
Walker James	Goffstown	"	P	McConnell's	19	"	175
Wallace James	Bedford	"	P	"	19	"	177
Wallace John	"	"	P	"	19	"	175
Wells Reuben	"	"	P	"	19	"	176

1, 2, 3, 4, 5, 7, 8, 9, 10 — At Bunker Hill.
6 — Killed.
    Webster Israel, Welch Moses, of Salisbury, Webster's Co., enlisted August 25, 1777.   Vol. 15, 166.
    Wesson Ephraim, Post's Co., enlisted September 1, 1777.   Vol. 15, 153.

9

Name.	Residence.	Regiment.	Rank.	Company.	Enlisted.	Vol.	Page.
Wheeler William Jr	Dunbarton	Stickney's	P	McConnell's	July 19	15	176
Whitehouse Solomon	Pembroke	"	P	"	19	"	175
Willet Joshua	Weare	"	P	"	19	"	177
West Gilman	Concord	"	P	Kimball's	20	"	187
Whittemore Aaron	Lyndeborough	"	P	Clark's	21	"	188
Wilson Robert	New Boston	"	P	"	21	"	189
Woodbury Nathaniel	Lyndeborough	"	P	"	21	"	188
Woodbury Josiah	"	"	P	"	21	"	188
Watson Samuel		"	Corpl	Gilman's	20	"	191
Wentworth Nathaniel	Middleton	"	Lieut	"	20	"	191
Wentworth John	Wakefield	"	P	"	20	"	191
Wentworth Henry		"	P	"	20	"	191
Wiggin James	Wolfeborough	"	P	"	20	"	192
Willey Samuel	Wakefield	"	P	"	20	"	191
Wood James		"	P	"	20	"	192
Webster Nathaniel	Gilmanton	"	P	N Wilson's	22	"	194
Wilson Nathaniel	"	"	Capt	"	22	"	194
Walker Abel	Charlestown	Hobart's	Capt	Walker's	21	"	143
Walker Seth	"	"	Ensign	"	21	"	143
Walker Nathaniel		"	P	"	21	"	145
Weed Benjamin	Charlestown	"	P	"	21	"	143
Willard Willoughby	Acworth	"	P	"	21	"	144
Woods Joseph	Claremont	"	P	"	21	"	144
Woodward Daniel	Sunapee	"	P	"	21	"	144
Waldo Edward	Alstead	"	Lieut	Webber's	21	"	146
Wardner Jacob	"	"	P	"	21	"	147
Watts John	"	"	P	"	21	"	147
Webber Christopher	Walpole	"	Capt	"	19	"	146
Willey Allen	Lempster	"	P	"	21	"	147
Wilcox Uriah	Newport	"	Lieut	"	21	"	146
Wood Samuel		"	P	"	21	"	147
Willoughby John Jr	Plymouth	"	P	Elliot's	21	"	150
Wyatt Daniel	Campton	"	P	"	21	"	149
Weare Joseph	Orford	"	P	Post's	24	"	153
Wesson Aaron	Haverhill	"	P	"	24	"	153
Woodworth Roswell	Lyme	"	P	"	24	"	153
Warren Aaron	Croydon	"	P	Hendee's	23	"	156
Warren Moses	"	"	P	"	23	"	156
Wells Ezekiel	Canaan	"	Sergt	"	23	"	155
Whitton John	Cornish	"	P	"	23	"	156
Williams Daniel	Plainfield	"	P	"	23	"	155
Wilson Isaac	"	"	P	"	23	"	155
Wood Joseph Jr	Lebanon	"	P	"	23	"	156
Woodbury Nathan	Croydon	"	P	"	23	"	156
Woodward Titus	Jefferson	"	P	"	23	"	157
Young John	Peterborough	Nichols's	Surg'n		23	"	198

Name.	Residence.	Regiment.	Rank.	Company.	Enlisted.	Vol.	Page.
Young Jotham – [1]	Canterbury	Stickney's	P	Sias's	July 20	15	180
York John	Wakefield	"	Sergt	Gilman's	20	"	191
York David		"	P	"	20	"	192
Young Thomas		"	P	"	20	"	192
Young Hezekiah	Unity	Hobart's	P	Walker's	21	"	144
York Christopher	Claremont	"	P	"	21	"	144
Young Joshua	Haverhill	"	Fifer	Post's	24	"	152

1 — At Bunker Hill.

Page 29, reference 1, at Bunker Hill; killed at Bennington.

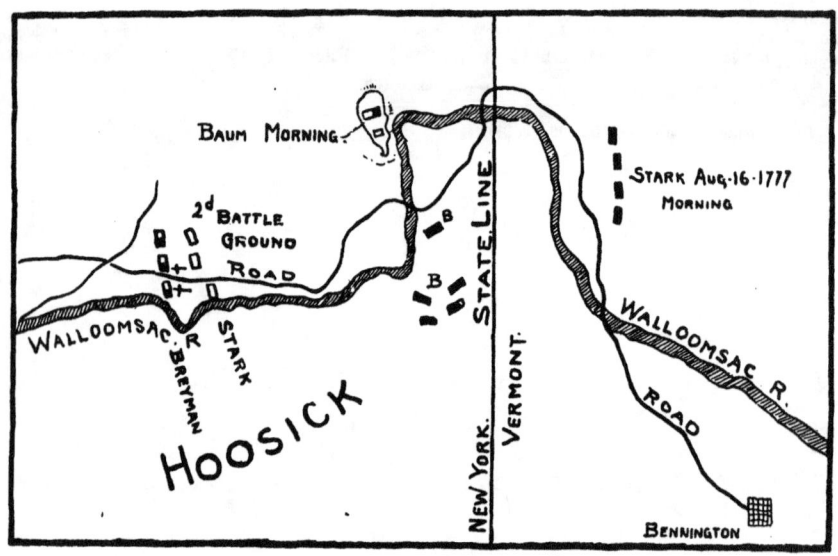

DIAGRAM OF THE BATTLEFIELD AT BENNINGTON.

APPENDIX.

To the memory of the brave New Hampshire men who lost their lives, from 1775 to 1782, in maintaining the right of self government, and whose bones lie mouldering beneath the sod of nearly every battlefield of the Revolution.

The records are lamentably deficient, and if ever made are now lost. This roll apparently does not contain one half the names of the men lost in this army of three regiments, enlisted for three years, or for the war. Of six companies, no returns are found. Colonel Cilley's regiment returns 18, Colonel Reid's, 14, and Colonel Scammel's 131 men as killed or died of disease during the three years.

As this roll will probably be published in a larger work contemplated by the compiler, he would be pleased to hear from any person having a knowledge of missing names, or any corrections of the residence as now given.

Address,

GEORGE C. GILMORE,

Manchester, N. H.

10

APPENDIX.

Name.	Residence.	Rank.	Casualties.	Date.	Year.	Remarks.
Abbot Ebenezer	Mason	P	Died	July 15	1778	
Adams Isaac	Rindge	P	Killed	June 17	1775	
Adams Winborn	Durham	Col	"	Sept 19	1777	
Adams Peter	Surry	P	Died	Aug 8	1778	
Aiken James	Chester	P	"		1780	
Aiken James Jr	"	P	"	Mar 1	1776	
Alley Daniel	Rochester	P	"		1777	
Amsden Joel	Henniker	P	"	May 25	1775	Ward's Mass. Reg.,
Ashley Daniel	Walpole	P	"	Aug 1	1781	[Fay's Co
Austin John		P	"	Aug 20	1777	
Bailey Benjamin	Nashua	P	"	Oct 7	1776	
Bailey William	Salisbury	P	"	Mar 1	1778	
Baldwin Isaac	Hillsborough	Capt	Killed	June 17	1775	
Baker Samuel	Newmarket	P	"	Oct. 7	1777	
Barnet William	Bedford	P	Died			
Bates Nathaniel	Dublin	P	Killed	Sept 19	1777	
Batchelder Josiah	Deerfield	P	"	July 3	1777	
Batchelder Stephen	"	P	Died	Nov 2	1777	
Batchelder Nathaniel	"	Sergt	"	Mar 24	1778	
Beal Zachariah	Portsmouth	Capt	Killed	Nov 8	1777	
Bell Frederick M	Dover	Capt	Died	Oct 9	1777	From wounds
Bemaine George	Henniker	P	Killed	Oct 28	1776	
Berry John	Chester	P	"		1777	
Bickford Joseph	Hopkinton	P	Died	June 29	1778	
Blake William	Moultonborough	P	Killed	May 12	1778	
Blake Henry		P	Died	Nov 30	1777	
Blake Joshua	Hampton Falls	Fifer	"	Mar 15	1778	
Blaisdell Ebenezer	Hampton	P	"	Aug 15	1777	
Blodget Thomas	Stratford	P	Killed	Oct 24	1777	
Blood Joseph	Mason	P	"	June 17	1775	
Blood Ebenezer Jr	"	P	"	June 17	1775	
Blood Nathan	Hollis	P	"	June 17	1775	Prescott's Mass. Reg.,
Blood Josiah	"	P	Died	Sept 16	1776	[Dow's Co
Blood Daniel	"	P	"	Nov 28	1778	
Bonney Jacob	Surry	P	"	July	1778	[Dow's Co
Boynton Jacob	Hollis	P	Killed	June 17	1775	Prescott's Mass. Reg,.

Name.	Residence.	Rank.	Casualties.	Date.	Year.	Remarks.
Bradshaw Patrick		P	Died	Feb 15	1776	
Bradford Joseph	Amherst	Lieut	"	July	1775	
Bradbury Saunders	Hudson	P	"		1779	
Brewer Peter	Amherst	P	Killed	Oct 7	1777	
Briggs Nathaniel	Keene	P	Died	Oct 18	1777	From wounds
Broderick Joseph		P	Killed	June 17	1775	On Roll, June 17
Brown Silas	Plymouth	P	Died	Dec 10	1777	
Bunker Joseph	Barnstead	P	"		1781	
Burton William	Wilton	P	"	Aug 1	1778	
Burns Philip	Hampton Falls	P	"	Nov 16	1777	
Butterfield Zachariah	Rumney	P	Killed	Aug 16	1777	
Caldwell Paul	Londonderry	P	"	June 17	1775	
Callahan John	Bedford	P	"			
Cairy Peter		P	Died	Apr 16	1776	
Carleton David	Lyndeborough	P	"	June 19	1775	From wounds
Carleton George	Rindge	P	Killed	June 17	1775	
Carr Elias	Kingston	P	Died	Mar 20	1778	
Carr Daniel	Hampton Falls	P	"	Jan 1	1778	
Carkin Isaac	Lyndeborough	P	"	Dec	1781	
Chamberlain Benjamin		P	"	June 25	1775	From wounds
Chandler Primus	Bedford			May	1776	Taken prisoner and
Chandler (Abiel)	Concord	Capt	Died	Sept 17	1776	[never heard from
Chandler Peter		P	"	Feb 18	1776	
Chase Nathaniel	Meredith	P	Killed		1781	
Church Iddo	Gilsum	Sergt	"	Sept 19	1777	
Cilley Daniel		P	Died	Jan 5	1777	
Clark Josiah	Nottingham	P	"			
Clark James	Amherst	P	"	July	1776	
Clayes Elijah	Fitzwilliam	Capt	"	Nov	1779	From wounds
Clifford Abraham	Rye	P	Killed			
Clogston Paul	Nashua	P	Died	July 15	1775	From wounds
Cochran Robert	Amherst	P	"			
Cochran Jonathan	"	P	"	Mar 24	1778	
Coffin Eliphalet	Exeter	P	"	Jan	1776	
Cogan Patrick	Durham	Q M	"	Aug 22	1778	
Cobb Isaac	Westmoreland	P	Killed	Aug 29	1778	
Cole John	Amherst	P	"	June 17	1775	
Colby Eli	Alexandria	P	"	Aug 16	1777	
Colby Isaac		P	"	Aug 27	1778	
Colby Stephen	Warner	P	"	Nov 2	1781	
Colburn Andrew	Marlborough	Lieut Colonel	"	Sept 19	1777	
Colburn Thomas	Nashua	P	"	June 17	1775	Prescott's Mass. Reg.,
Colbath	Durham	P	Died			[Moore's Co
Collins Thomas	Windham	P	Killed	June 17	1775	
Cook Thomas	Campton	P	Died	Aug 7	1777	
Comstock Azariah	Richmond	Corpl	Killed	Sept 19	1777	

Butler Levi, Putney, Vt. Died March 30, 1778.

Name.	Residence.	Rank.	Casualties	Date	Year.	Remarks.
Comstock Josiah	Gilsum	P	Died	Jan 8	1779	
Conant Joshua	Londonderry	P	"	Sept 19	1777	
Coneck James – 1	Brookline	P	"	July 24	1775	From wounds
Connor Samuel	Pembroke	P	"	Oct 9	1777	From wounds
Conroy John Jr	Hollis	P	"	Sept	1778	
Cram Asa	Wilton	P	"	Sept 10	1775	
Crawford John	Hill	P	"	Oct 12	1777	From wounds
Cromwell Eliphalet	Somersworth	P	Killed	July	1777	
Crosby Jonathan	Greenland	P	Died	Nov 1	1777	
Cross Ralph Jr	Bow	P	"	Dec	1776	
Crown William	Durham	P	"	July 15	1777	
Cummings Abraham	Greenland	P	"	Sept 24	1777	
Cummings Ebenezer	Hollis	P	"	Mar 7	1778	Small pox
Cummings Reuben	Merrimack	Drum	"	Sept 13	1776	Only 16 years old
Cunningham Archibald	Londonderry	P	"	Aug 28	1777	From wounds
Dalton Caleb		P	Killed	June 17	1775	
Daniels Nathaniel	Lee	Corpl	Died	Mar 8	1778	
Dame Jonathan	Rochester	P	"	Nov 16	1777	
Davis John	Chesterfield	P	Killed	June 17	1775	
Davis Joseph	Amherst	P	"	Aug 13	1779	
Davis Ezekiel	"	P	"	Aug 16	1779	Killed previous to
Davis Samuel		P	Died	April 6	1780	[Aug 29
Davis Isaac	Kingston	Sergt	"	July 8	1777	
Day Stephen	Keene	P	"	Oct 6	1775	From wounds
Dearborn Thomas	Candia	Lieut	Killed	Aug 30	1778	
Dearborn Abner	.	P	Died	Sept 2	1779	From wounds. Only
Dearborn Samuel	North Hampton	Sergt	"	July 13	1778	[16 years old
Demery John Jr	Rindge	P	Killed	Nov 1	1781	
Dickey William	Londonderry	P	"	Aug	1778	
Dickey James	Antrim	P	"	Oct 28	1776	
Dike Benjamin	Amherst	P	"	Oct 7	1777	
Dinsmore Samuel	Chester	P	Died		1776	
Dodge William	Winchester	P	"	Sept 30	1777	From wounds
Dole John	Jaffrey	P	Died	Mar 15	1782	
Dolloff Joseph	South Hampton	P	"	Sept 3	1777	
Door John	Amherst	P	Killed	Oct 7	1777	
Dow Thomas		P	Died		1777	
Drury John	Temple	Fifer	Killed	July 28	1778	
Dudley Joseph	Epping	P	Died	May 15	1777	
Durgin Benjamin	Durham	P	"	Mar 7	1778	
Dwyer John	Allenstown	P	"	July 7	1777	
Eastman Collins	Hopkinton	P	Killed	Oct 7	1777	
Eastman Caleb – 2	Groton	P	"	June 19	1775	Accidentally killed

1 — Prescott's Mass. Reg., Gilbert's Co.
2 — Prescott's Mass. Reg., Dow's Co.
　　Cleaveland Acquilla, Guilford, Vt. Killed June 17, 1777.
　　Coffin Michael, Cavendish, Vt. Died March, 1780.

Name.	Residence.	Rank.	Casualties.	Date.	Year.	Remarks.
Eastman Samuel	Walpole	P	Died	Aug 24	1778	
Eaton Benjamin	Meredith	Drum	"		1777	
Emerson	Chester	P	"		1778	
Facy Joseph	Walpole	Lieut	"	Nov 2	1777	
Farwell Joseph	Charlestown	P	Killed	June 17	1775	
Farmer Minot	Hollis	Sergt	Died	May 9	1776	Prescott's Mass. Reg.,
Fellows Samuel	Danville	P	"	Sept 15	1778	[Dow's Co
Fifield Stephen	Brentwood	P	"	Sept 3	1777	
Fisk Solomon	Concord	P	"	Aug 10	1778	
Fisk Ephraim	"	P	"	Mar 1	1776	
Fisk James	Hollis	P	"	May 29	1775	Prescott's Mass. Reg.,
Flagg James	Sandwich	Sergt	"	Sept 24	1777	[Dow's Co
Flanders Stephen	Goffstown	P	"	Oct 24	1777	
Forsaith David	Chester	Lieut	"	May 10	1778	
Forsaith Jonathan	"	P	"		1777	
Foss Richard	Brentwood	P	"	Aug 12	1777	
Foss George	Barrington	P	"	Nov 30	1777	
Fox Joel	Campton	P	"	June 1	1777	
Frankford William	Swanzey	P	"	Apr 17	1779	
Freeman Frederick	Marlborough	P	Killed	Oct 7	1777	
French William	Nelson	P	"	June 17	1775	
Fuller Joshua	Surry	P	"	Aug 16	1777	
Fuller Ezra	Temple	P	Died	July 1	1778	
Fuller Amos	"	P	"	July 14	1778	
Fullerton Jonathan	Raymond	P	Killed		1777	
Gage Andrew	Salem	Corpl	Died	July 10	1778	
Garland John	Rochester	P	"	May 10	1778	
George Josiah	Hampton	P	"	Sept 20	1778	
Gibson James	Goffstown	P	Killed	July 7	1777	
Gilman John	Wakefield	P	Died	Mar 15	1778	
Glidden Peter		P	"	Nov 18	1777	
Glines Nathaniel	Canterbury	P	"	Feb 18	1776	
Goff William	Bedford	P	Killed			
Gordon David		P	Died	May 4	1778	
Gordon Joseph	Exeter	P	"	July 20	1778	
Goss Richard	Rye	Sergt	Killed	Oct 7	1777	
Goodenough Calvin	Marlborough	P	Died			
Goodman Richard	Amherst	P	"	June 27	1778	
Gray Jonathan	Wilton	P	"		1775	
Greeley Benjamin	Hudson	P	"	Sept 7	1775	
Greeley Reuben	Salisbury	P	"	April 1	1778	
Griffin Dominicus	Deerfield	Corpl	"	Mar 15	1778	
Griffin Richard	Plymouth	P	"	July	1778	
Hackett George	Salisbury	P	"	Nov 30	1780	
Hale Nathan	Rindge	Col	"	Sept 23	1780	A prisoner

Fuller Jonathan, Drummer, Westminster, Vt. Killed September 19, 1777
Gould Nehemiah, Westminister, Vt. Died August 10, 1778.

Name.	Residence.	Rank.	Casualties.	Date.	Year.	Remarks.
Hale Thomas	Plaistow	P	Died		1777	
Hall Ziba	Keene	Corpl	"	June 30	1779	
Hall James	Lee	P	"	Mar 8	1778	
Hall Benjamin	"	P	"	Mar 10	1778	
Hall James Jr	Nottingham	P	"	Mar 12	1778	
Hamilton Samuel	Londonderry	P	Killed	July 5	1777	
Handsom John	Rindge	P	"	Aug 3	1777	
Hanson Joshua	Dover	P	Died	Oct 23	1777	
Haskell Abijah	Rindge	P	"	July 26	1778	
Hastings James	Canterbury	P	"	Sept 28	1777	
Hastings Robert	"	P	"	Sept 29	1779	
Heath Zebedee	Sandown	P	"		1777	
Heath Ephraim	Salisbury	P	"	Mar 26	1778	
Heath Richard	Hampstead	P	"	July 10	1778	
Hills Parker	Candia	P	Killed	June 17	1775	
Hix Barnard	Richmond	P	Died		1776	
Hobart Isaac	Hollis	P	Killed	June 17	1775	Prescott's Mass. Reg.,
Hobart Solomon	Plymouth	P	"	Aug 16	1777	[Dow's Co
Holland Nathaniel	Meredith	P	Died	Apr 22	1778	
Holden James	Wilton	P	"	Aug 29	1776	
Holmes John Jr	Campton	P	"	Dec 1	1777	
Honey Calvin	Amherst	P	"	Dec 15	1781	
Honey John	Wilton	P	"	Oct 24	1776	
Hooper Thomas	New Boston	P	"	Aug 25	1777	From wounds
Houston Caleb	Rindge	P	"	Nov 5	1776	
Howe Jonas	Marlborough	P	Killed	June 17	1775	
Howe Charles	Portsmouth	Drum	"	July 3	1777	
Hoyt Thomas	Canterbury	P	Died	Sept 1	1778	
Hoyt William	Exeter	P	Killed	July 5	1777	
Hull Samuel	Plymouth	P	Died	Sept 8	1777	
Hull Nathaniel	"	P	"	Sept 6	1777	
Huckins Stephen	New Durham	P	"	Aug 28	1780	
Hunter	Jaffrey	Lieut	"	Oct 25	1776	
Huntress Jonathan	Newington	P	Killed	Aug 29	1779	
Hutchinson James	Amherst	P	Died	June 24	1775	From wounds
Hutchinson James	Temple	P	"	June 27	1778	
Jackson Clement Jr	Portsmouth	P	"	Dec 31	1777	
Jackson Daniel	Madbury	P	"	Nov	1778	From wounds
Jenness Job	Rye	P	"	Nov 15	1777	
Jewett Joseph	Sanbornton	P	"	Sept 1	1777	
Johnson William		P	"	Aug 26	1777	
Johnson Timothy	Concord	P	"		1777	
Johnson Calvin	Bedford	P	"			
Jones Lloyd		P	"	June 1	1777	
Jones William	Amherst	P	"	Oct 9	1776	
Kemp Solomon	Bedford	P	Killed			Mass. Reg
Kendall Edward	Rumney	Sergt	Died	June 15	1778	
Kenniston Winthrop	Epping	P	"	Mar 15	1782	

Name.	Residence.	Rank.	Casualties	Date.	Year.	Remarks.
Kenney Amos	Hudson	P	Killed	Oct 7	1777	
Kentfield Shem	Marlborough	P	Died	June	1782	"Hanged"
Kimball Benjamin	Plaistow	P M	Killed	Aug 23	1779	Accidentally killed
Kimball Obadiah	Concord	P	"	Oct 7	1777	
Kincaid John	Windham	P	"	Aug 16	1777	
Knight Caleb	Atkinson	P	Died	July 1	1778	
Knowles Samuel	Rye	Corpl	"	June 16	1778	
Lampson Jeremiah	Amherst	P	"	Aug	1776	
Lane Ezekiel	Raymond	Lieut	Killed	Aug 16	1777	
Lane Nathan	" "	P	Died	Sept 26	1776	
Larry Stephen	Newcastle	P	"	July 6	1778	
Lawrence Joseph	Walpole	Lieut	"	June 4	1777	
Lear William	Middleton	P	"	July 4	1778	
Leeland Isaac	Rindge	P	Killed	Sept 3	1777	
Leeman Samuel Jr	Hollis	Lieut	"	July 7	1777	
Leighton Joseph	Newington	P	Died	Nov 13	1777	
Lewis Asa	Milford	P	Killed	Aug 16	1777	Then Duxbury school
Lewis John	Portsmouth	P	"	Dec 26	1776	[farm
Lewis Joseph	Wilton	P	Died	July 25	1778	
Locke Abner		P	"	Aug 17	1778	
Locke Orson	Kensington	P	Killed		1779	
Lovejoy Jonathan	Rindge	P	"	June 17	1775	
Lowe David	Pelham	P	Died	Dec	1780	
Lucas Elijah	Plymouth	P	"	Sept 1	1777	
Lufkin William		P	"	Mar 1	1778	
Magoone John	Sanbornton	P	Killed	Sept 19	1777	
Marden William	Greenland	P	Died	Dec 1	1777	
Marden Samuel	Rye	P	"		1775	
Manual John	Bow	P	Killed	June 17	1775	
Mansfield Elijah	Temple	P	Died	May 19	1778	
Marston Jonathan	North Hampton	P	"	Sept 30	1777	
Marston John	" " .	P	"	June	1777	
Martin Sidon	Lee	P	"	Nov 12	1777	
Marsh Christopher	Campton	P	"	Sept 28	1777	
Mason John	Epsom	P	"	Oct 25	1777	
Mason Benjamin	Nottingham	P	"	June 30	1778	
Matthews Thomas	Bedford	P	"	Mar 16	1781	
McAffee Samuel	"	P	"	Aug 18	1777	From wounds
McBritton William Jr	Sunapee	P	"		1779	From wounds
McCarr Daniel	Rindge	P	"	Jan 1	1778	
McCarty Charles	Goffstown	Fifer	Killed	Oct 7	1777	
McCauley Nathaniel	Litchfield	Lieut	"	Aug 29	1779	
McClary Andrew	Epsom	Major	"	June 17	1775	
McClary Michael	"	Capt	"	Oct 7	1777	
McClary David	Londonderry	Lieut	"	Aug 16	1777	
McClary John	Deerfield	Lieut	Died	Nov 26	1777	
McCrillis William	Nottingham	P	"	July 2	1775	From wounds
McDonald John	Londonderry	P	"	July 1	1777	

Name.	Residence.	Rank.	Casualties.	Date.	Year.	Remarks.
McGrath Daniel – [1]	Amherst	P	Died	Aug 10	1775	From wounds
McIntosh Archibald – [2]	Brookline	P	"	Aug 10	1775	From wounds
Melvin John		P	Killed	June 17	1775	On roll, D^d June 17
Metcalf Michael	Keene	P	"	Aug 16	1777	
Minot Joseph	Hollis	P	"	June 17	1775	Prescott's Mass. Reg.
Mitchell William	Concord	P	"	June 17	1775	[Parker's Co
Mixer Nathan	Fitzwilliam	Sergt	"	Aug 16	1777	
Moore John	Candia	P	Died	Aug 21	1777	
Moorland William	Salem	P	Killed	Oct 7	1777	
Murphy John	Hampton	P	"	Oct 7	1777	
Myrick Ezra		P	Died	Sept 28	1777	
Neal Ebenezer	North Hampton	Corpl	"	Dec 1	1777	
Needham Nathaniel	Wilton	P	"		1779	
Newland Jonathan	Westmoreland	P	"	Jan 11	1778	
Newton Thomas	Kingston	P	"	Sept 1	1777	[Dow's Co
Nevins Phinehas	Hollis	P	Killed	June 17	1775	Prescott's Mass. Reg.
Nevins David	Plymouth	P	Died	Feb	1778	Died a prisoner
Nevins William	Hollis	P	"		1776	
Nims Asahel	Keene	Sergt	Killed	June 17	1775	
Oliver Aaron	Temple	P	Died	Apr 30	1778	
O'Sullivan Valentine	Bedford	P	Killed	July 7	1777	
Page Timothy	Atkinson	P	Died	Sept 26	1777	
Palmer Zadoc		P	"	July 30	1778	
Parker James	Portsmouth	P	"	May 17	1778	
Parker Benjamin	Swanzey	P	Killed	Sept 19	1777	
Parker Josiah	Wilton	P	Died	Oct 22	1776	
Parker Thomas	Portsmouth	P	"	Apr 9	1777	
Parsons William		P	"	Aug 25	1779	
Patten James		P	Killed	June 17	1775	On roll, D^d June 17
Peabody Thomas		Surg'n	Died	Nov 20	1777	
Peavey Edward	New Durham	P	"	July 14	1777	
Perry Ebenezer	Wilton	Lieut	Killed	Aug 16	1777	
Perry Samuel	Hampstead	P	Died	Nov 1	1777	
Perry Thomas	Bradford	P	"		1780	
Perry Jonas	Wilton	P	"	Sept 30	1777	
Phillips Benjamin	Plymouth	P	"	Oct 12	1780	
Pierce Asa	Wilton	Sergt	"	June 27	1780	Drowned
Pidge Henry	Fitzwilliam	P	"	Sept 29	1775	Ward's Mass. Reg.
Pike Dudley		P	"	Nov 30	1777	[Barnes's Co
Pitman Joseph	Madbury	P	"			
Platts Abel Jr	Rindge	P	"		1777	
Plumer Jabez		P	"			From wounds
Pomp Peter	Epsom	P	"	Mar 15	1778	

1 — Mass. Reg., died a prisoner.
2 — Prescott's Mass. Reg., Gilbert's Co., prisoner.
   Newton Jonas, Guilford, Vt. Died September, 1777.
   Owen Benjamin, Hartford, Vt. Died, 1778.

Name	Residence.	Rank.	Casualties.	Date.	Year.	Remarks.
Porter Joseph	Chesterfield	P	Died	Apr 27	1778	
Poor Enoch	Exeter	Genl	"	Sept 8	1780	
Poor Moses		P	Killed	June 17	1775	[Dow's Co
Poor Peter	Hollis	P	"	June 17	1775	Prescott's Mass. Reg.,
Post Jeremiah	Orford	Capt	Died	Aug 26	1777	From wounds
Powers Francis G	Hollis	P	Killed		1780	
Prescott John	Raymond	P	Died		1776	
Prescott Edward		Corpl	"	Nov 1	1777	
Proctor Jeremiah	Stoddard	P	"	Aug 23	1777	From wounds
Putnam Caleb	Wilton	P	"	Aug 22	1776	
Ramsey David	Amherst	P	"	Dec 2	1775	
Randall James Jr	Newcastle	P	"	July 22	1778	
Ranstead John	Westmoreland	P	Killed	Aug 16	1777	
Rawlins Benjamin	Epping	Corpl	Died	July 15	1777	
Rawlins Moses	Exeter	P	"	Nov 30	1777	
Rawlins John	Greenland	Corpl	Killed	Oct 8	1777	
Rice Peter	Keene	P	Died	Nov 20	1781	
Rice Joel	Cornish	P	"		1776	
Richardson Nathaniel	Stoddard	P	"	June 24	1777	Only 16 years old
Ritter Daniel	Walpole	Sergt	"	Sept 1	1779	
Roberts Thomas	Somersworth	P	"	July 19	1775	
Rowen Andrew	Canterbury	P	"	Mar 1	1778	
Runnels Isaac	Barrington	Lieut	"	Nov 15	1777	
Russ James	Chester	P	Killed		1777	
Russell Jason	Nashua	P	Died	Sept 10	1775	Reported dead
Russell Isaac	Wilton	P	"	Sept 15	1776	
Sawyer Nourse	Wilton	P	"	July	1776	
Scammell Alexander	Durham	Adjutant General	"	Oct 6	1781	From wounds
Scott David	Peterborough	P	Killed	June 17	1775	
Shackford Seth R	Newington	Sergt	"	Oct 7	1777	
Shannon George	Canterbury	P	"	June 17	1775	
Shattuck Jeremiah	Hollis	P	Died	May 29	1775	Prescott's Mass. Reg.,
Shattuck Isaac	"	P	"		1776	[Dow's Co
Shattuck William	Amherst	P	"	June 30	1777	
Shepard Roswell	Alstead	P	"		1776	Of small pox
Shortridge Richard	Portsmouth	Capt	"	July 8	1776	
Sinclair Ebenezer	Weare	P	Killed	Oct 7	1777	
Smiley William Jr	Jaffrey	P	Died		1776	
Smith Joseph	Brentwood	P	"	Mar 1	1778	
Smith John		P	"	Mar 1	1778	
Smith John	Richmond	P	"	Nov	1780	Drowned
Smith Samuel		P	"	Sept 14	1777	
Snow Daniel Jr	Keene	P	Killed	Oct 7	1777	
Spencer Asa	Campton	P	Died	Mar 7	1778	
Stanyan Jonathan	Chichester	Lieut	"	Nov 11	1777	
Stevens Abial	Tamworth	Corpl	"	Oct 20	1777	From wounds

Perry James, Westford, Mass. Died April 3, 1780.

12

Name.	Residence.	Rank.	Casualties.	Date.	Year.	Remarks.
Stevens Phinehas	Tamworth	P	Died	Apr 21	1778	
Stevenson Philip	Dover	P	"	July	1781	
Stone Josiah	Temple	P	Killed	Sept 19	1777	
Straw Benjamin	Sandown	P	Died	Sept 1	1778	
Taggart John	Peterborough	Lieut	Killed	July 7	1777	
Tate Mark	Somersworth	P	Died		1777	
Taylor Benjamin	Amherst	Capt	"	Feb	1776	
Taylor Thomas	Sanbornton	P	"	Aug 25	1777	
Taylor John Jr	Stratham	P	Killed	July 3	1777	
Taylor Joseph	Peterborough	P	"	June 17	1775	
Thomas Joseph M	Deerfield	Lieut	"	Sept 19	1777	
Thornton Hugh	Bedford	P	Died		1778	
Thompson Samuel Jr	Londonderry	P	"		1780	Small pox
Tisdale Benoni	Westmoreland	Fifer	Killed	Aug 16	1777	
Towne Archelaus	Amherst	Capt	Died	Dec 1	1779	
True Samuel	Hampstead	S M	"	Aug 5	1778	
Tuck William	Amherst	P	"			
Tucker John	Epping	P	"		1782	
Tuck Samuel	Hampton Falls	Lieut	"	Nov 12	1777	
Turrill Joshua	Deerfield	P	"	Oct 25	1777	
Tuttle Thomas	Weare	P	"		1778	
Upton Aaron	Amherst	P	"	Dec	1776	
Veazey Eliphalet	Stratham	P	"		1779	
Wait Joseph	Claremont	Col	"	Sept 13	1776	From wounds
Walden Thomas	Portsmouth	P	"	June 20	1777	
Wadleigh Abraham	Exeter	P	"	Aug 10	1777	
Wallingford Samuel	Dover	Lieut	Killed	Apr 24	1778	
Ward Richard	Portsmouth	P	Died	May 12	1778	
Warren Benjamin	Winchester	Corpl	Killed	Sept 19	1777	
Weare Richard	Portsmouth	Capt	"	Aug 4	1777	
Webster Amos	Plymouth	Lieut	"	Oct 7	1777	
Webster Abel Jr	"	P	Died	July	1778	
Wells Josiah	Chester	P	"			
Wesson Isaac	Jaffrey	P	"	Apr	1779	
Wheat Thomas Jr	Hollis	P	Killed	June 17	1775	Prescott's Mass. Reg.,
Wheeler Lebbeus	"	P	Died	July 10	1778	[Dow's Co
White James	Portsmouth	P	"	July 25	1778	
Whitney Thomas		P	"	Oct 1	1778	
Wilder Thomas	Keene	P	"		1776	Small pox
Wilder Nathaniel	Winchester	P	"	Sept 30	1777	
Willoughby Josiah	Plymouth	P	"	Dec 31	1777	
Wilson Joseph	Rindge	P	Killed	Aug 16	1777	
Winslow Elisha	Sandwich	P	Died	July 6	1779	Drowned
Wilkins Daniel Jr	Amherst	P	"	July	1776	
Wilkins William H	"	P	"	June 22	1778	
Wilkins Sylvester	"	P	"	Sept 20	1779	

Name.	Residence.	Rank.	Casualties.	Date.	Year.	Remarks.
Wood Oliver	Nashua	P	Died	Sept 10	1775	Reported Sept 10
Woodbury Levi	Amherst	P	"			Died a prisoner
Woods William	Keene	P	Killed	Aug 16	1777	
Worthen Samuel	Weare	P	Died	Nov 10	1777	
Wright Ebenezer W	Amherst	P	"	Nov	1775	
Wyman Abel	Pelham	P	"	Sept 11	1781	
Young Nathaniel	Lisbon	P	"	July 19	1775	[Moore's Co
Youngman Ebenezer	Hollis	P	Killed	June 17	1775	Prescott's Mass. Reg.,

Wiman James, Woburn, Mass. Died August 17, 1775.

Page 47 — Joseph Broderick, P, killed June 17, 1775. On Roll, " D⁴ June 17."

The names of Vermont and Massachusetts men, in foot notes, killed or died of disease, were soldiers in New Hampshire Regiments.

The running title, " New Hampshire Soldiers at Bennington," should have been omitted from pages 47 to 55 inclusive of the appendix.

ROLL

OF

NEW HAMPSHIRE MEN

AT

LOUISBURG, CAPE BRETON,

1745.

JOINT RESOLUTION TO AUTHORIZE THE GOVERNOR AND
COUNCIL TO APPOINT A PERSON OR PERSONS TO
REPRESENT THE STATE OF NEW HAMPSHIRE AT THE
PROPOSED CELEBRATION AT LOUISBURG.

[$500 appropriated.]

*Resolved by the Senate and House of Representatives in
General Court convened:*

That the governor and council are hereby authorized to
appoint a person or persons to represent the state of New
Hampshire at the proposed celebration of the one hundred
and fiftieth anniversary of the capture of Louisburg, to be
held at Louisburg June 17, 1895. Such representative or
representatives shall receive their actual expenses only, and
the same shall be paid from any money in the treasury not
otherwise appropriated, upon approval of the governor and
council. The governor and council are hereby further
authorized to cause to be printed not exceeding two thousand copies of the report of such representative or representatives, together with the names of the soldiers from
New Hampshire who served at the capture of Louisburg,
and all of the historical facts connected therewith, the same
to be distributed as follows: One copy to each representative and senator of the New Hampshire legislature, one copy
to each state officer, one copy to each Grand Army post in
the state, one copy to each town library in the state, and
the balance to be deposited in the state library and disposed
of by the trustees thereof in the same manner as other
publications deposited therein. The total expenditure
under this resolution shall not exceed five hundred dollars.

[Approved March 28, 1895.]

Session Laws of 1895, chapter 138.

His Excellency
CHARLES A. BUSIEL, Governor,
AND THE HONORABLE COUNCIL,

Appointed the writer special commissioner to represent New Hampshire at the proposed celebration at Louisburg, Cape Breton, June 17, 1895, collect the historical facts, names of the New Hampshire soldiers and sailors in the expedition, and cause the same to be published.

After one hundred and fifty years have come and gone since the events took place, with the loss of all the muster rolls and many other documents that would throw light on the subject, I find the best explanation of the situation by Hon. Charles Hudson of Lexington, Mass., in the New England Genealogical and Antiquarian Register, Vol. 24, 367 : " Every antiquary who has attempted to explore that field must have been disappointed in not being able to find a list of the gallant men who served in the memorable expedition to Cape Breton in 1745, when the undisciplined militia of New England took Louisburg from the veteran troops of France. It will be recollected that that expedition originated with the colony, and was executed by colonial troops. The bravery displayed and the complete success which crowned the enterprise attracted attention across the Atlantic, so that the mother country readily assumed the act and paid the cost of the expedition. To adjust these accounts it became necessary that they should have the rolls, and they were accordingly sent to England, and have never been returned. In fact, the same is true of the records of the council of that day; they were sent to the home government, and the copies now in the archives of the state are transcripts from the original records. No such copies of these rolls have ever been made, and hence our archives furnish no lists of these brave men. Feeling the great need of some such list, I have endeavored to collect from all sources within my reach, the names of the officers and soldiers who served in that campaign. But I have found the task more difficult than I anticipated. In the first place, but few of the lists I have been able to find give the residence of the officers or soldiers, so that in many cases it is difficult to determine even to what state certain men or detachments belong. Neither do the lists I have been able to find profess to be full or perfect. In fact they are not properly rolls of the companies. They are, rather, partial reports of the sanitary condition of certain detachments at particular stations, or of the men assigned to a particular command, or the signers of petitions for a certain object, or the names of those who empowered a certain person to act as their agent in receiving their bounty or share of the spoils. In some cases we have only the notice that such an one is in the hospital, or is dead, or is discharged for inability. I have thought it due to the public to make this statement, that they may see how much dependence may be placed upon the lists I propose to give. I cannot say that they are perfect, or entirely reliable, but only that I have used my best endeavors to make them as perfect as my means would allow, and I flatter myself that my labors have not been entirely in vain."

This description of the situation of affairs by Mr. Hudson applies as well to New Hampshire as to Massachusetts. The number of men from New Hampshire in the expedition when it sailed for Louisburg was 502. Recruits, 120 at least, and probably more. Have found the names of 496 men, leaving 126 unaccounted for. The residences of the men, as given, are the writer's.

The writer is under great obligations to Senator Gallinger, who called the attention of Secretary Olney to the missing muster-rolls and, through him, of Minister Bayard in England, where the rolls undoubtedly went as vouchers, although no clue to them has been obtained there yet.

We hope our members of congress, with the assistance

of the delegations from Massachusetts, Rhode Island, and Connecticut, will secure an appropriation from the government to enable further investigations to be made, and, if possible, to obtain copies of the rolls, in order that justice may be done to the memory of the brave men who captured Louisburg.

GEORGE C. GILMORE,

Special Commissioner.

Manchester, N. H., Sept. 25, 1896.

The provincial government of New Hampshire in 1745 consisted of a royal governor, council, and assembly.

Governor.

BENNING WENTWORTH.

Council.

George Jaffrey,
Jotham Odiorn,
Henry Sherburne,
Joseph Sherburne,
Ellis Huske,
Theodore Atkinson,
Samuel Solley,
John Downing,
Richard Wibird,
Samuel Smith.

Assembly.

Province of } Anno Regni Regis Georgii Secundi, Magnæ
New Hamp^r } Brittaniæ, Franciæ et Hiberniæ, Decimo Octavo, &c.

A Journal of the House of Representatives at a General Assembly of his Majesty's Province of New Hampshire in

New Engl^d began and held at Portsm° in s^d Province on Thursday 24 January, Anno Dom: 1745.

Portsm°	Nathaniel Rogers, Esq Eleazer Russell, Esq Henry Sherburn, jun.
Dover	Coll. Thomas Wallingford Thomas Millet, Esq. Capt. John Winget
Hampton Hampton Falls	Saml Palmer, Esq. Mr. Joseph Philbrook Mr. Meshech Wear
Exeter	Col. Peter Gilman Mr. Zeb. Gideons
Stretham	Moses Levitt, Esq.
New Castle	William Frost, Esq.
Rye	Jonathan Lock
Kingston	Maj^r Eben^r Stevens, Esq.
Greenland	Clement March, Esq.
*Newington	George Walton, Esq.
New Market	Capt. Israel Gilman
Durham	Capt Jonathan Thompson
Londonderry	Mr John Wallace, Sen

Friday Feby 1. Declared by the House, not legally elected, and dismissed.

Feby 12. Mr. Secretary, Coll. Downing & Mr. Wibird came into the House & declaring they were sent to qualify John Fabyan, Esq. adminis^d the oath to him, & he took his place in ye House being directed thereto by the speaker.

Journal of the House.

Fryday, Feby 1st 1745. Met according to adjournm^t & all ye members present.

Richd Wibird Esq. brought down a letter from his Exc^y Govr Shirley with some papers Relating to the proceedings of the Gov^t of the Mass. Bay on an intended Expedition to Louisburg.

* Elected to fill the vacancy caused by the dismissal of George Walton, Esq.

Governor Shirley's Communication.

Province of the }
Massachusetts Bay }

The Committee of both Houses upon the subject of his Excellency's messages of the 19th & 22[d] instant make the following report, viz.

That they have been attended by two Gentlemen who have lately been prisoners at Louisburg & by others who have been traders there & who are well acquainted with the place, from whom the Committee have received information that the Garrison there does not consist of more than five or six hundred regular Troops & that there are not above three or four hundred fighting men of the Inhabitants, that they have but a small stock of Provisions, that they have no vessels of Force in their Harbour, and that the place is at this time less capable of being defended against an attack than its probable, it will be hereafter.

The Committee therefore are of opinion that it is incumbent upon this Government to embrace this favourable opportunity to attempt the reduction thereof; and they humbly propose that his Excell[y] the Capt. General be desired to give forth his Proclamation to encourage the Inlistment of three Thousand Volunteers under such proper officers as he shall appoint, That each person so enlisting be allowed Twenty-five shillings pr month, & that there be delivered to each man a blanket, that one month's pay be advanced & that they be entitled to all the plunder.

That provision be made for the furnishing of necessary warlike stores for the Expedition, That four months provisions be laid in, That a Committee be appointed to procure & fit vessels to serve as Transports to be ready to depart by the beginning of March, and that a suitable naval force be provided for their convoy, as this Court shall hereafter order. That application be forthwith made to the Government of New York, the Jerseys & Pennsylvania, New Hampshire, Connecticutt & Rhode Island to furnish their respective

Quotas of men & vessels to accompany or follow the Forces
of this Province.

In the name & by order of the Committee.

Wm. Pepperell.

In Council, Jan. 25, 1745—Read & Sent down.

In the House of Represent⁵, Jan, 25, 1745—Read & Accepted.   Sent up for concurrence.

T. Cushing, Speakʳ.

In Council, Jan. 25, 1745—Read & concurred.

J. Williard, Secʸ.

Consented to

W. Shirley.

Copy examinᵈ pr. J. Williard Secʸ.

Saturday, Febʸ yᵉ 2ᵈ 1745.   Met according to adjournment & the Comᵗᵉ of both Houses on the subject of Govʳ
Shirleys letter & some other papers laid before the House
yesterday by his Excʸ having made their Report, it was
brought into the House by Mr. Downing & Mr. Solly & read
as follows:

Province of New Hampʳ.

The Committee of both Houses on the subject of his
Excellency Governor Shirleys letter and some other papers
laid before the Assembly this day by his Excellency:

The Committee are of opinion that it is incumbent upon
this Province to do all they can to forward & encourage
the intended Expedition for the Reduction of Louisburg or
Cape Breton, and humbly propose that (if proper methods
may be concluded on for defraying the charge which the
Committee are of opinion will be about four thousand
pounds lawfull money) his Excellency the Captain General
be desired to give forth his Proclamation to encourage the
enlisting of two hundred & fifty volunteers under such
proper officers as he shall appoint; that each person so enlisting be allowed Twenty-five shillings pr month & that
be delivered to each man a blanket, that one months pay be
advanced and that they be entitled to all the plunder ; That

provision be made for the furnishing of necessary warlike
stores for the Expedition, that four months provision be
laid in, that a Comittee be appointed to procure & fit ves-
sells to serve as transports to be ready to depart by the
beginning of March.

Feby 1, 1745—   Theodore Atkinson   Peter Gilman
                  Saml Smith   Thos Millet
                  John Downing   Hen. Sherburne
                  Saml Solly.   Moses Leavit.

Voted, That afores^d Report of Com^tee be accepted & sent
up for concurrance.

Cape Breton Expedition—Plan of Operations*.

MEM°. In order for the attacking of Louisbourg this
Spring by surprise its propos'd that 3000 Troops should
Embark from hence in Sloops & Schooners and proceed for
Canso, well armed which should be a place of Rendezvous
it being within 20 Leagues of Louisbourg; and its being
uncertain that so many vessels should be able to keep Company together when they are arrived at said Port, to take a
favourable opportunity to sail from thence in order to be at
Gaberous point by Dusk, from whence it is but 3 Leagues
from Louisbourg, then to push into the Bay, and as soon as
said vessels are at an anchor to man as many whaleboats as
they have & send them along the shore as neare as possible.
which will make it the more difficult for them to be discov-
ered, & when they come to the cove which faces the low
part of the wall, there to land if the Sea will permit & scale
that place if possible, & if otherwise as the Wall breaks off
a little on the other side of the East gate, not far from that
there are picketts put for a considerable distance across a
pond over to the Wall on the Beach on the other side of
the Pond, and as this Pond is frozen all the month of March
its not very difficult to get over them : but if the weather

*This paper was laid before the House, with the letter from Governor Shirley.

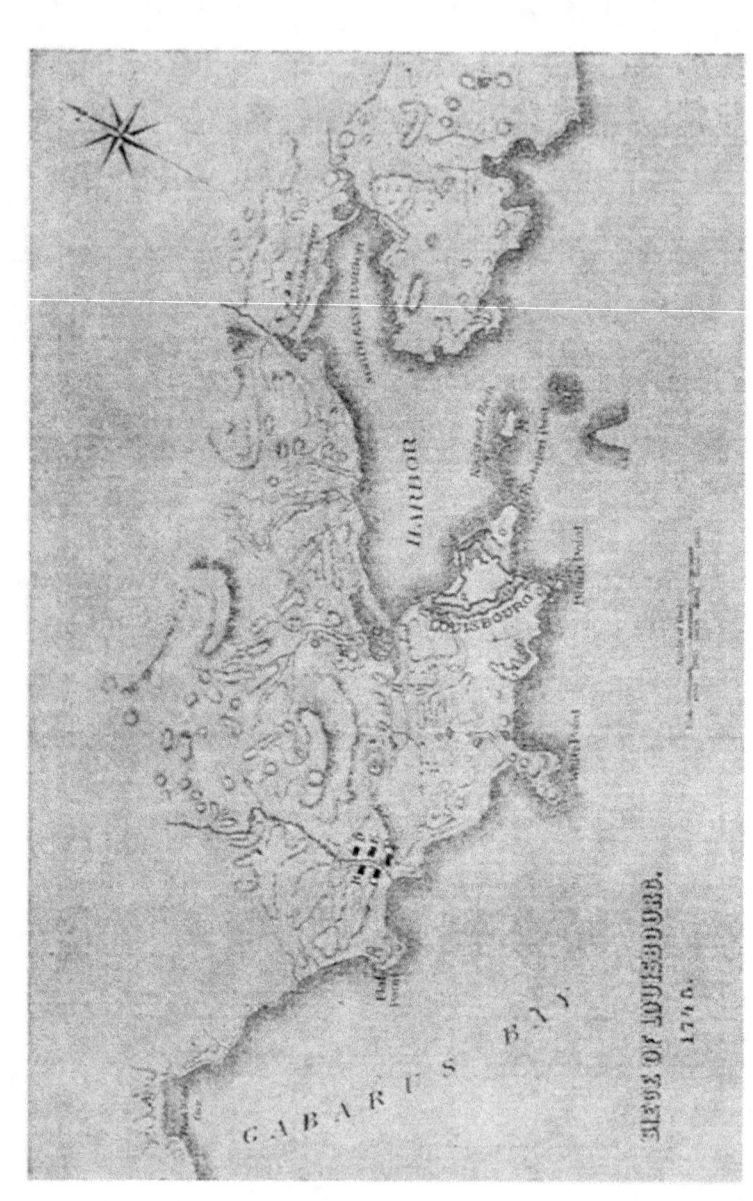

SIEGE OF LOUISBOURG.
1745.

INDEX

TO MÅP OF THE SIEGE OF LOUISBOURG, 1745.

A Landing of New England Men.

B Camp of Burr's Regiment.

C   "   " Pepperrell's "

D   "   " Willard's   "

E   "   " Moulton's   "

F   "   " Moore's   "

G First or Green Hill Battery.

H Second Battery.

I Third Battery.

J Fourth, or Advanced Battery.

K Fifth, or Titcomb's Battery.

L Lighthouse Battery.

M Island Battery (French).

N Grand, or Royal Battery (French).

O Burying-ground.

P King's Bastion, or Citadel.

Q Barachois.

R West Gate.

S South Gate.

T Maurepas Gate.

will not permit their landing in the above place let them proceed along the shore till they come to a long Range of Rocks that goes towards the Island, at the End of which is a Passage where the shallops go through, let them go in there and follow the Ledge of Rocks right back again, then they will land right against the East gate on a point, and as there are some Houses there, it will hinder their being seen, but one Boat ought to go first & surprise the People in those Houses a little time before the others come up, Each whale boat must have two ladders in them fifteen foot long which may be put in the middle of the Boat without hindrance to the men ; but the Boatmen must lay still at this Point till they think the main body is got near the Town, & that a party of as many men as shall be judg'd proper shall be ready to attack the Grand Battery, its necessary it should be low water if no Drift Ice aground along the shore, for the remainder of the men to go round the Picketts that are by the north gate, and when they get round with Ladders of 15 feet long, they can scale the Wall facing the Harbour which is a Quarter of a mile round, and it will be absolutely necessary to appoint a Time to strike the blow all at once, which can be done by agreeing upon a certain hour just before Day, which is the Sleepiest Time, and the Commanding officer of each Detachment to know the time, and when the Time comes by his Watch to begin without further ceremony ; The Enemy finding themselves attacked at so many different places at once its probable it will breed such confusion among them that our men will have time to get in unmolested ; & it is to be observ'd that as the men march from the above point the low wall is on the left hand of the gate, and the Picketts on the right hand ; as all the enemy's troops are in the citadel except a small guard or two it will be a considerable time before the men are drest & got ready to march out, and even then it is quite in the other End of the town.

This is what probably may succeed, but least any accident

should happen to prevent it, it will be necessary to provide accordingly & in case our People should be discover'd & Repuls'd the above number of men being sufficient to command the field, it will be necessary in order to reduce the place to have what shipping can possibly be got to cruise off the Harbour's Mouth in order to intercept their Provision vessels which they Expect early being at this time very short of Provisions, as likewise to take any transports with men if any should come, and that our men may not be discourag'd at being repuls'd once, it will be necessary to send 12 nine pounders & two small mortars with shells, &c. and a Quantity of Provisions, so to bombard them & endeavor to make Breaches in their Walls & then storm them: and should the shipping be so lucky as to take their Provisions and the land forces take all their cattle & keep them constantly employed, it will be impossible for them to hold the place till the last of July for want of provisions.

In order the better to secure the Retreat in case a superiour naval Force to ours should come from France & drive ours off the Coast, it will be necessary to have two small vessels with about Two hundred men at Canso, & the day after the Fleet is sail'd for Louisbourg for them to sail so as to get in by night, and it being but six Leagues from Canso to St. Peters they can get there before day & surprise that place, which is an exceeding good harbour for small vessels, but has not Water sufficient for vessels of that size which will be able to drive ours off the Coast, so that the vessels for the Retreat will lay there safe, and the Troops be able to go to them by Land; there will be an advantage besides this in surprising this place as there is always a number of Indians with their Families which keep with a French Priest at a small Distance from the French Inhabitants, and the Booty taken there will pay the Expence & more in taking it. It is to be observed that during the time our Troops lay siege to the Town, it will be in their power to send parties and Destroy all their Fishery on the

Island as well as the north side of the Harbour which would ruin their Fishery for four or five years; and as it is impossible to fail of taking the Royal Battery at least, that would in a great measure lay open their Harbour exposed unto an attack by Sea from England, as the new Batterys in the Town in the greatest part of the Ambrozers, there are no guns & there are two gates that are made in Diamond fashion facing the Harbour that can be beat down in an instant the peices not being but 2 inches & an half thick.

N. B. The full complement of Troops is 700 out of which deductions must be made of 50 for each of the two Batteries, viz. the Royal & Island Batteries, & 50 for Death, sickness &c. which reduce them to 550, and the other fighting men in the Town do not exceed 300, and that the Swiss Troops which are their best Troops are exceeding Discontented & mutinous; also that at St. Peters there may be about 200 men in scatter'd houses, and in the suburbs of the Town of Louisbourg without the Walls about 200. it is improbable that more than two 30 or 40 Gun ships should come with Mr. Duviver who may be expected the first with Recruits & supplies, and in case the naval Force that comes should be superiour to our naval Force, that our 3000 men would command the Field, & continue so till they could be protected & Reinforc'd from England.

Indorsed, "Cape Britton
Expedⁿ—Plan of operation, Feby 1, 1745—"

His Exc^y sent down ye following written Message by Coll. Downing & Mr. Solly:

Gentlemen of the Assembly,

In consequence of your message of the 2^d Inst. I express'd a messenger to Boston in order to get the Proclamations necessary to be Dispersed throughout the Province for encouraging the Expedition to Louisburgh printed, which I have this moment received, & as soon as the sheriff attends on me shall order them to be dispersed.

B. WENTWORTH.

Council Chamber, In Portsm° Feby 5th 1745.

Message of His Excellency.

Gentlemen of the Assembly,

By your message of this day, I find the disposition of the House is to augment the forces to Louisburgh to four or five hundred men, sailors included, which is very pleasing to me; and if the House will send up a Resolve on that subject & in what manner they propose to pay the Expence, it will facilitate the other bill that now lays before me, which at present appears very difficult;—but by no means put off the augmentation or the charge to a further day.

Council Chamber in   B. WENTWORTH.
Portsm° Feby 12, 1745—

February 14, 1745, Mr. Secretary came down with the following Message from his Exc^y: His Ex^{cy} recomends it to the House to pass a vote that the officers & soldiers in y^s Province for the Expedition agst Louisburg have ye same pay as in the Massachusetts, wch he apprehends would be for the encouraging the affairs going on.

Voted That the Collonel, Lt. Collonel & Major, Captains & all under officers that are or shall be appointed to command the voluntiers voted by the Genl Assembly to go on the Expedition agst Louisburg have the same allowances made them pr month as are allowed by the Government of the Mass: Bay on ye s^d Expedition, provided each Company consists of forty men or upwards, & that the Captains have the same allowance for enlisting men in proportion to the number of men in each Company & that no Capt. be entitled to the bounty for enlisting men untill his Company be compleated;

Voted, That the same encouragement be given to private Centinalls & sailors that will enlist as voluntiers on ye Exped^n agst Louisburgh as is given in ye Prov. of Mass^s Bay,

Establishment of the officers' Pay in Massachusetts on the Expedition against Louisbourgh, 1745.

Generall pr month	£15 :
Collonell	12
Lt. Coll	10
Major	8
Adjutant	4 : 10
Capt.	4 : 10
Lieut	3
2ᵈ Lieut	2
Sergent	1 : 10
Corporal	1 : 8
Clerk	4
Surgeon Genˡˡ	5
Under Surgeon	4 : 10
Drum Major	1 : 12
Comon Drumʳ	1
Chaplain	4 : 10
Capt of yᵉ Artillery	9
Lieut	4 : 10
Qr. Gunner	2
2 Bombarders	4
Do Assistance	1 : 12
Armorer	1 : 12

Incouragement for the men that Inlist, viz.

To each man besides what is mentioned in the Proclamation by way of Bounty, old Tenor,	£4 :
To Billiting money from the Time of Inlisting pr. week to pay from the time of Inlisting	1 :
To each Capt. over & above his pay for his Expences in Visiting his Company, old Tenʳ	25 :

Further to Incourage men to Inlist it is proposed that the Widows or nearest relatives of any offcer or soldier that is slain or shall otherwise loose his life in the service, shall be entitled to four months pay.

And that the wives of any officer or soldier in the Expedition or any other person that appears with a power of Attorney duly authenticated, shall at the end of every month receive out of the Treasury half or all the wages of such officer or soldier as he appears for which will greatly encourage the present Expedition.

Boston Feby 26, 1745.

Sir—

I am extremely glad to hear of your good prospect of completing your Regiment in time: All things will be ready here for the Imbarcation of our fleet by the end of the week as the committee informs me, so I should be glad of your being ready with yours as soon as may be; whatever you want for the 150 men to go wth my commissions & in the pay of this government, be pleased to send to me for it by Express and you shall have it instantly.

I think the essential thing is the number of men in the whole; and y^t it is not absolutely necessary y^t there should be exactly 50 men in each company, if there are 40 in one and 60 in another, all the things may be set right by proportioning the service in the field; and indeed if a company does not consist of less yⁿ 40 men I think we ought not to be critical.

I am wth much & respect
y^r Excelencys most
Obedient humble servant
W. SHIRLEY.

His Exc^y. Govr Wentworth.

Boston, March 27, 1745.

Sir—

I should have mentioned y^t this morning Donahoe sail'd with another sloop under his convoy having on board a company of 50 men to reconnoitre the Coast, &c. and to clear it agst the arrival of the Fleet, and if it should happen y^t your Transports should get the start of ours, I am advis'd y^t it would be safest for 'em to stop at Whitehead Harbour ab^t 5 or 6 Leagues short of Canso, till the arrival of ours y^t there may be as little danger as is possible of occasioning intelligence being convey'd to the Enemy by any little vessell to the Eastward of Canso, wch may discover 'em; and if you approve of it I shall be glad if you order it accordingly. I am inform'd y^t Mr. Sparhawk has got some very good cutlasses and some firelocks wch it is doubted are not extraordinary: If you will be pleas'd to take the trouble of appointing some skillfull person to view both of 'em, and in case they or either of 'em are approv'd of, desire him to put such as are approv'd on board one of your Transports for the use of our Troops as spare arms, I shall be oblig'd to you, and our Committee will pay him for 'em. But if they are not good I would not have 'em. We forgot to put up among the Stores for our 150 men in your Regiment Gunpowder and Ball: If you will be pleas'd to supply 'em with three half barrels of powder and a like proportion of Ball for their passage, I shall be oblig'd to you, and will repay you by the first opportunity; The Blankets and money not used be pleas'd to return by a convenient opportunity. I must beg the favour of you to indulge Mr. Bollan in his Inclos'd request, if no inconvenience will attend it. I have so much fatigue y^t I wth great difficulty hold out, but not without having impair'd my health.

God send us both a good riddance of our Trouble and an happy Event to the Expedition.

I am sincerely,

Your Exc^{ys} faithfull, humble servant

W. SHIRLEY.

To his Exc^y Gov. Wentworth.

2

Boston May–13–1745

Sir

As to the agreement your Excellency mentions to be made between you and me, that the Companies to be rais'd in your Government should consist of 40 men each, and that three companys of 50 men each should at all Events be rais'd by you to be in the pay of this Government & added to your companies, I am apt to think may be a mistake.

It is certain that I always intended and understood the agreement to be that you should if you pleas'd raise as many men to be in the pay of this Province as would make up your 350 a Regiment of 500 men.

I can't pretend to recollect every expression which may have dropped from my pen on this affair between us; But I am satisfied the agreement you mention is so foreign to my intention that upon perusing my letters again and comparing 'em with your own you will find the real agreement to be, that all the men not exceeding 150 to be raised by you over and above the Quota of 350 Voted by your Assembly, should be paid and subsisted by this Government. The reason of my mentioning to you the vote of the Assembly of this Province for reducing our Companies from 50 men in each to 40, was to remove the difficulty of their first vote which I was afraid might ly in your way as it did in mine here, by which no Captain that had not raised 50 men was entituled to have his Company received into pay; whereas by the second vote fourty men was to be received as a Company, which I found an ease to me in raiseing my own Levies, but whatever I have said in that respect was not designed in the least as a proposal or agreement that your Companys should be only eight in number and consist of no more than 40 men Each, and that at all events this Province was to pay & subsist 150 men of New Hampshire Regiment. But upon the whole I ever understood that this Government was to pay and subsist as many men not exceeding 150 as you should raise within your Province over and above your own Governments Quota of 350 & no more.

I am with great respect

Sir—your Excellencys most obedient

humble servant

W. SHIRLEY.

His Exc^y Govr Wentworth.

The New Hampshire Adjutant-General's Report, Vol. 2, 1866, contains the rolls of the seven companies in Colonel Moore's regiment, over his own signature, dated at Louisburg, November 20, 1745. The adjutant-general quotes Dr. Belknap, as follows:

"Thus, Dr. Belknap states that Col. Moore's regiment consisted of eight companies, when the return of his regiment, over his own signature, shows but seven companies."

We think the following letter of Governor Wentworth will show the eighth company, as it was one of the companies not returned by Colonel Moore.

Letter from His Excellency Benning Wentworth, Esq., Governor of New Hampshire, to Lt. General Pepperell.

March 28^d 1745.

SR.

I herewith transmitt to you a List of the Transports employ'd by this Government for the service of the Expedition against the French at Louisburg, also what Transports are employ'd to transport the one hundred & fifty men, in the pay of the Massachusetts Government, which are aggregated to the Regiment, whereof I have appointed Saml Moore, Esq. Colonel. Also I think proper to acquaint you that I have appointed Capt. Fernald Commander of a Sloop fitted out by this Government, in a warlike manner, to annoy his Majesty's Enemies, and to guard and convoy the Transports. I have also appointed the said Jn° Fernald a Capt of a Company in Col. Moore's Regiment to act either by Land or by sea, as the service may require it. I have thought it necessary, in order to preserve the Command you are appointed to, that you have the intire command and disposition of the Regiment and Transports, also of the Sloop of War, And I do hereby put the same absolutely under your command, hereby requiring them to obey you, as their Commander-in-Chief, and to follow such orders and commands as from time to time they or either of them shall receive from you.

Sr—yʳ Hum : servᵗ

B. WENTWORTH.

Lieutenant-general William Pepperell, of Kittery, Me., was commander-in-chief of the land forces, sailors, and marines on board the transports and the armed vessels that convoyed the troops to Louisburg—the total number of men, probably 4,000, and all furnished by the provinces of New Hampshire, Massachusetts, Connecticut, and Rhode Island.*

Governor Wentworth's proclamation for enlisting soldiers and sailors for the Louisburg expedition not on record, or copy known to be in existence.

Off for Louisburg.

After two months' discussion of measures by the Assembly and Council, then in session at Portsmouth, to raise men and money to defray expenses, the expedition was ready, and sailed from Portsmouth March 23ᵈ O. S., or April 4ᵗʰ N. S., 1745—several days before the Massachusetts troops left Boston. The New Hampshire regiment was 500 strong, under the command of Col. Samuel Moore, of Portsmouth; eight companies, and probably three com-

---

* Did not arrive at Louisburg until after the fort was captured.

panies (150 men) of New Hampshire in the pay of Massachusetts, in Colonel Moore's regiment. On this point there has been a wide diversity of opinion, as there is not, as far as is now known, a single muster or pay-roll in existence. It was customary at that time in the English service for the field officers to have command of companies as colonel and captain at the same time. In order to substantiate my view that there were eleven companies in Colonel Moore's regiment, of 45 men to each company, the names of all the commissioned officers, date of commission, and date of discharge, are given, all the others being recruits, after the capture of Louisburg, June 17, 1745.

Names.	Rank.	Date of Commission.	Date of Discharge.
Moore, Samuel,	Colonel.	Feb. 12, 1745.	Aug. 15, 1746.
Meserve, Nathaniel, 2d,	Colonel.	Feb. 13, 1745.	Nov. 11, 1745.
Gilman, Ezekiel,	Major.	Feb. 13, 1745.	Nov. 11, 1745.
*Mason, John T.,	Captain.	Feb. 13, 1745.	July 31, 1745.
Seaward, William,	Captain.	Feb. 13, 1745.	Nov. 10, 1745.
†Fernald, John,	Captain.	Feb. 13, 1745.	Nov. 11, 1745.
Sherburne, Henry,	Captain.	Feb. 13, 1745.	June 28, 1745.
Ladd, Daniel,	Captain.	Feb. 13, 1745.	Sept. 4, 1745.
‡Hale, Samuel,	Captain.	Feb. 13, 1745.	July 15, 1746.
Whidden, James,	Captain.	Feb. 13, 1745.	Nov. 10, 1745.
Waldron, Thomas W.,	Captain.	Feb. 13, 1745.	Sept. 6, 1745.
Dudley, Trueworthy,	Captain.	Feb. 13, 1745.	July 21, 1745.
Tilton, Jacob,	Captain.	March 1, 1745.	Nov. 11, 1745.
Williams, Edward,	Captain.	March 2, 1745.	Feb. 6, 1746.
§Wise, John,	Captain.	April 15, 1745.	No date.
Sherburne, Joseph,	Captain.	June 6, 1745.	June 30, 1746.

Lieutenants.

Names.	Rank.	Date of Commission.	Date of Discharge.
Hart, John,	Lieutenant.	Feb. 13, 1745.	July 31, 1745.
Leavett, Samuel,	Lieutenant.	Feb. 13, 1745.	Sept. 6, 1745.
White, Samuel,	Lieutenant.	Feb. 13, 1745.	Oct. 9, 1745.
‖Flagg, John,	Lieutenant.	Feb. 13, 1745.	Sept. 30, 1745.

* No company; independent command.
† Captain of armed sloop Abigail.
‡ Promoted to major Oct. 16, 1745.
§ Captain of armed sloop.
‖ Promoted to captain. No date.

Daniels, Eliphalet,	Lieutenant.	Feb.	13, 1745.	July	31, 1745.
Foss, Zachariah,	Lieutenant.	Feb.	13, 1745.	Nov.	14, 1745.
Wheelwright, Jeremiah,	Lieutenant.	Feb.	13, 1745.	Sept.	22, 1745.
Dudley, James,	Lieutenant.	Feb.	13, 1745.	Aug.	7, 1745.
Wingate, Moses,	Lieutenant.	Feb.	13, 1745.	Sept.	30, 1745.
Mattoon, Richard,	Lieutenant.	Feb.	13, 1745.	Nov.	11, 1745.
Robie, Samuel,	Lieutenant.	Feb.	13, 1745.	Sept.	30, 1745.
Connor, Samuel,	Lieutenant.	Feb.	13, 1745.	July	31, 1745.

Ensigns.

Names.	Rank.	Date of Commission.		Date of Discharge.	
*Newmarch, Thomas,	Ensign.	Feb.	13, 1745.	June	20, 1746.
†Brown, Edmund,	Ensign.	Feb.	13, 1745.	July	1, 1746.
Tufts, Thomas,	Ensign.	Feb.	13, 1745.	Sept.	6, 1745.
Wormall, Daniel,	Ensign.	Feb.	13, 1745.	Nov.	11, 1745.
‡Pitman, Ezekiel, Jr.,	Ensign.	Feb.	13, 1745.	Nov.	10, 1745.
Huntress, Christopher,	Ensign.	Feb.	13, 1745.	July	31, 1745.
Brooks, Edward,	Ensign.	Feb.	13, 1745.	July	31, 1745.
Pickerin, Thomas,	Ensign.	Feb.	13, 1745.	Aug.	7, 1745.
Sleeper, Joseph,	Ensign.	Feb.	13, 1745.	Sept.	22, 1745.
Ham, Clement,	Ensign.	Feb.	13, 1745.	Sept.	30, 1745.
Perkins, Robert,	Ensign.	Feb.	13, 1745.	July	31, 1745.

The above-named officers were commissioned by Benning Wentworth, the governor of the province of New Hampshire.

Lieutenant-general Pepperell, at Canso, April 15, commissioned Abraham Trefethen, captain; Jonathan Gilman, lieutenant; Philip Yeaton, ensign.

Recruits.

Friday–June–8–1745.

The House met according to adjournment.

Voted, That Eleazʳ Russel Esq. Mr. Henry Sherburne jun. & Thoˢ Bell Esq. be a Comᵗᵉᵉ of this House to join with such as may be appointed by yᵉ Honᵇˡᵉ Council to consider of yᵉ subject matter of his Excelʸ Govʳ Shirly & Lieut. Genˡ Pepperells Letters relating to a Reinforcement

* Promoted to lieutenant Oct. 5.
† Promoted to lieutenant Oct. 1.
‡ Promoted to lieutenant June 20.

of our army at Louisburg & to consider what is proper for this Province to do & to make Report to the Gen¹ Court as soon as may be.

The Com^tee for considering the subject matter of his Exc^y Govr Shirlys & Lieut Gen¹ Pepperrells Letters relating a Reinforcement of the Army before Louisburgh, report as follows:

The Com^tee are humbly of opinion that (when proper methods may be agreed upon by the Gen¹ Assembly for defraying the charge) his Exc^y the Capt. Gen¹ be desired to issue forth his Proclamation for the Encouraging the enlisting of one hundred voluntiers under such proper officers as he may think proper to be employ'd in the Expedition against Louisburgh giving them the same Encouragement as was given to ye last voluntiers inlisted for said Expedition.

Prov. of   In ye House of Represent June   Jotham Odiorn
N. Hampr 10th 1745, Read and accepted & R. Wibird   Com-
       sent up for concurrence   Saml Solly   mittee
                                      Eleazr Russell
                                      Hen. Sherburne
                                      Thos Bell

Wednesday June 12th 1745.

The House met according to adjournment.

Mr. Secretary Atkinson came into the House & inform them that ye vote on Louisburgh Expedition, Com^tees Report for one Hund^d men were concurr'd & assented to by the Governor.

Tuesday July 2^d 1745.

The House met according to adjournment.

Mr. Secretary bro't into ye House a written message from his Excellency representing the Probability of 20 men being raised more than are voted for & Desiring to know whether ye House would have them Embark'd &c. and then the House adjourned for two Hours.

His Excellency's Message.

Gentlemen of the Assembly

It is very probable that about twenty men more than what are voted to be raised for the reinforcement of our troops now before Louisburgh, may appear, in which case I shall be glad to have your Resolve whether it will not be expedient to Imbark them, as it will greatly relieve the Forces now there from the hard duty they have so long undergone.

I shall also be glad to have your mind signified whether it be your Intent to have the Reinforcement Imbarked in case news should arrive before Imbarkation of the reduction of Louisburgh.

B. WENTWORTH.

Council Chamber in
Portsmouth, July 2d, 1745.

Saturday July 6th 1745.

Met according to adjournment.

In answer to his Excllʸˢ message by Mr. Secretary to know yᵉ opinion of yᵉ House about sending the Reinforcement for the army at Cape Britton & whether if twenty men more than yᵉ hundred appear'd the House were willing they should be sent,

Voted, That the Reinforcement be sent away with all possible Dispatch & that if twenty men more or any smaller number appeared as voluntiers they also be sent with them at the publick expense.

———

Statement of the Condition of the Men at Louisburg, 1745.

To His Excellency the Governor, the Honorable the Council, and House of Representatives, of His Majesties Province of New Hampshire.—

As we are refer'd to, in the preceeding Memorial, to give further Information, touching the State of our Soldiers; and authorized thereby, to Sollicit the Honorable Court in

their behalf; we humbly crave Leave, to offer this, as a
Supplement thereto.—

Besides the almost Naked Condition of those of our
Troops, who went first to Cape Breton ; Some of them are
So enfeebled, by reason of the Length and Hardships of
the Siege, & for want of necessary Comforts, in the Time
of it, as renders them unfit for further Service, till Re-
cruited ; others are Languishing under Sicknesses, of
Various kinds, and most of them, are overrun with Lice,
for want of Change of Apparel, which renders their Case
still more uncomfortable, Whereupon, we humbly recom-
mend, those Poor but brave men, to your Excellency's &
Honour's wise, Just, and Compassionate Consideration,
Earnestly beseeching, that Such of them as desire it, may
be immediatly dismiss'd, and bro't back to their Native
Country, their Families, & Friends ; that it may never be
Said, they bravely fought themselves into a Prison ; for,
what Else can be Said of it If they are Compell'd to tarry,
after the Expedition is Ended, as we apprehend it is, and
that in a most Compleat and effectual Manner: For that,
His Excellencys Proclamation of the 2 of February Last,
proposed an Expedition, for the Reduction of the French
Settlements, on the Island of Cape Breton, & not for the
garrisoning of them ; and the Enlistment, was in Consequence thereof, (namely,) for Reducing, & not for garrisoning, and we humbly appeal, to your Excellency's &
Honors Judgment, whether, reducing and garrisoning, be
not two things, quite different, and Distinct from each
other ; and if so, whether the Troops of the first Embarka-
tion, mayn't demand a discharge, as a Right and Justice
due to them, instead of Solliciting for it, as an Act of
Grace.   But, on the other hand, if it Should be Said, that
by the Expedition was meant and intended, that Louisbourg Should be garrison'd (in case of Success,) by those
who should reduce it ; It may be Answer'd, that Such Intention, cant Rationally be Extended further, than till

other Troops, might be rais'd to relieve them ; and more than three Months, is already Pass'd, Since the Surrender; a Space doubly Sufficient for that Purpose.—

We take Leave further to Propose, that in Consideration, the Plunder (which was expected would be great,) turns out, to be but a very Triffle, they May have an additional Grant of Bounty, as a further Reward, of their Toil, Hazard, and Bravery, as the Massachusetts Troops have already had.—

As to those, whose Lot may be to tarry over the Winter, Whether by Choice, or Compulsion, (if any Should be Compell'd so to Do,) We humbly propose, that besides an Augmentation of their Wages, and a Grant of Apparell, and Bedding, Suitable for the Climate and Season ; they May have an Augmentation of their allowance of Rum & Molasses, to half a Pint of Each, for Each Man ⅌ Day, and a Couple of Quarts of Small Beer also, the Waters there, being exceeding bad, and very unwholesome to Drink : that there may be a Surplus of Stores, of all kinds, to be Purchased of the Commissary, at a Stated Price, and that there may be a Provision of Physic, as well as of Food & Cloathing; and that Each Cap' may have a Copy, of the Invoices of the Stores & Cloaths Sent for the Soldiers, with the Prices of those Commodities, that they may be Sent for Sale; that the Care, the Justice, & the goodness of the Honorable Court, may be made known to every individual Man.—

As the Season of the year is far advanced, and the Soldiers greatly distress'd ; Some For Want of a Discharge, and other for want of Necessarys and Conveniences, to make their Lives Comfortable, We humbly Pray, that what we have offered, may have the earliest Consideration & Dispatch, that is Possible.

And your Memorialists as in Duty bound Shall Ever Pray

T. W. Waldron

Jonathan Prescut

Portsmouth Sep' 24 1745

Miscellaneous.—Notes, prior to, during, and after the Siege of Louisburg.

It appears from Gov. Wentworth's proclamation, or enlistment papers to the captains, for the enlisting of soldiers, and sailors, no particular time was inserted for their discharge, after the surrender of the fortress, the men were clamorous for their discharge, and not being complied with, caused considerable trouble, some of them were held until the arrival of troops from Great Britain, May 24, 1746, when 1500 were released.

The Louisburg expedition cost the province of New Hampshire, as reported by a committee of the Assembly, June 3, 1747, 26,489 pounds, 16 shillings, 8½ pence, Proclamation money.

Great Britain reimbursed the Province of New Hampshire, 16,355 pounds sterling. The money arrived in Boston, Sept. 18, 1749. The British fleet, commanded by Commodore Peter Warren, arrived before Louisburg at the commencement of hostilities, with the following vessels of war :

Superb	60 guns.
Launceston	40 "
Mermaid	40 "
*—Vigilant	64 "
May 22—Princes Mary	60 "
" "—Hector	40 "
June 10—Chester	50 "
" 12—Canterbury	60 "
" "—Sunderland	60 "
" "—Lark	40 "
" "—Eltham	40 "

This immense fleet of vessels of war took no active part in the assaults on the fortress, with the exception of a few

*Captured from the French, and manned by New England sailors.

gunners, who went ashore to instruct Pepperell's men in the management of their batteries.

Capt. Edward Tyng was in command of the Massachusetts Colonial squadron of seven vessels, carrying 108 guns.

Capt. John Fernald, of Portsmouth, commanded the sloop Abigail, of 14 guns, that convoyed the New Hampshire troops.

Two sloops from Connecticut, 80 guns, one armed vessel from Rhode Island, 20 guns,* with one hundred and fifty soldiers.

Belknap's History of New Hampshire.

"The fortress of Louisburg was so strong as to called, The Dunkirk of America ; and had been twenty-five years in building, and cost 1,200,000 pounds Sterling.

"This expedition originated in Massachusetts, but the colonies of New Hampshire, Rhode Island, and Connecticut by their legislative authority, furnished troops and stores, New York sent a supply of artillery, Pennsylvania, and New Jersey, provisions and clothing." The assault on the Island battery, defended by 180 men, and 30 cannon, was disastrous to the 400 provincial troops who made the assault, nearly one half being either killed, drowned, or taken prisoners.

The French loss during the entire siege, is reported to have been 200 men.

When Duchambon, the Governor of Cape Breton, surrendered to General Pepperell, there was turned over to him, 1,900 prisoners, 125 large cannon, 19 mortars, stores of provisions, enough to last six months.

General Amherst, commanding the land forces, and Admiral Boscawen, of the British navy, captured Louisburg, July 26, 1758, and completely destroyed the splendid fortress, and it remains so to this date.

No enumeration of the number of the inhabitants of New Hampshire, was made until 1767, when there were 52,700.

*Did not arrive in Louisburg until after the fortress was taken.

The ratable polls returned in 1742 as 5,172, with Nottingham, Barrington, and Gosport, missing.   Call the number of ratable polls in 1745, 6,000, and multiply by 4.50, would give the number of inhabitants in New Hampshire in 1745 as 27,000.

France declared war against Great Britain March 15, 1744, N. S.

Great Britain declared war against France, March 29, 1744, O. S.

After the treaty of peace, October 7, 1748, Louisburg was turned over to the French intact, and the British troops evacuated Louisburg July 12, 1749.   And the provinces gained practically nothing for their blood and treasure expended during the war.

The pay of the soldiers in provincial currency was twenty-five shillings a month, or less than sixpence a day, sterling, the soldier furnishing his own clothing and gun.

From Parkman's, " A Half Century of Conflict ":

" The New England soldier fancied that he was doing the work of God.   And the descendant of the Puritans was never so well pleased as when teaching their duty to other people, whether by pen, voice, or bombshells.   The ragged artillerymen, battering the walls of papistical Louisburg, flattered themselves with the notion that they were champions of gospel truth.   Barefoot and tattered, they toiled on with indomitable pluck, doing the work which oxen could not do, with no comfort but their daily dram of New England rum."

" Maine, then a part of Massachusetts, furnished full one third of the men of the Massachusetts contingent."

According to Parkman, the winter of 1746 must have been terrible, on account of sickness, " At the end of January, five hundred, and sixty one had died "

" On May 10, 1746, Governor Shirley writes to Newcastle, that eight hundred and ninety men, had died during the winter "

From Douglas, North America:

" outside the Maurepas Gate, by the old lime-Kiln, the forgotten bones of above five hundred New England men lie there to this day, under the coarse neglected grass "

There is in the library of the New Hampshire Historical society at Concord, a book containing two hundred and sixty pages, inscribed as follows : " A List of Prisoners tryed at General Court Martial held at Louisburg, in the Island of Cape Breton, in the years 1746—1747 & 1748." And has the appearance of being, and undoubtedly is, the original journal.

The officers of the New Hampshire troops on their return home, presented a bell (which has since been re-cast) that they had captured at Louisburg, to Queen's Chapel, Portsmouth. The peal of the brazen-tongued messenger from the grim old fortifications of Louisburg is still heard from the tower of St John's church.

From Barstow's History of New Hampshire:

" Louisburg was situated on a neck of land south of one of the finest harbors on the island. The city was surrounded by a wall of stone thirty-six feet high."

William Vaughan of Portsmouth is said to have been the originator of the Louisburg expedition.

Not a man in the expedition had previously seen Louisburg.

Distance from Portsmouth to Louisburg about six hundred miles.

The city of Louisburg, at the time of its capture, contained 5,000 inhabitants, exclusive of the troops.

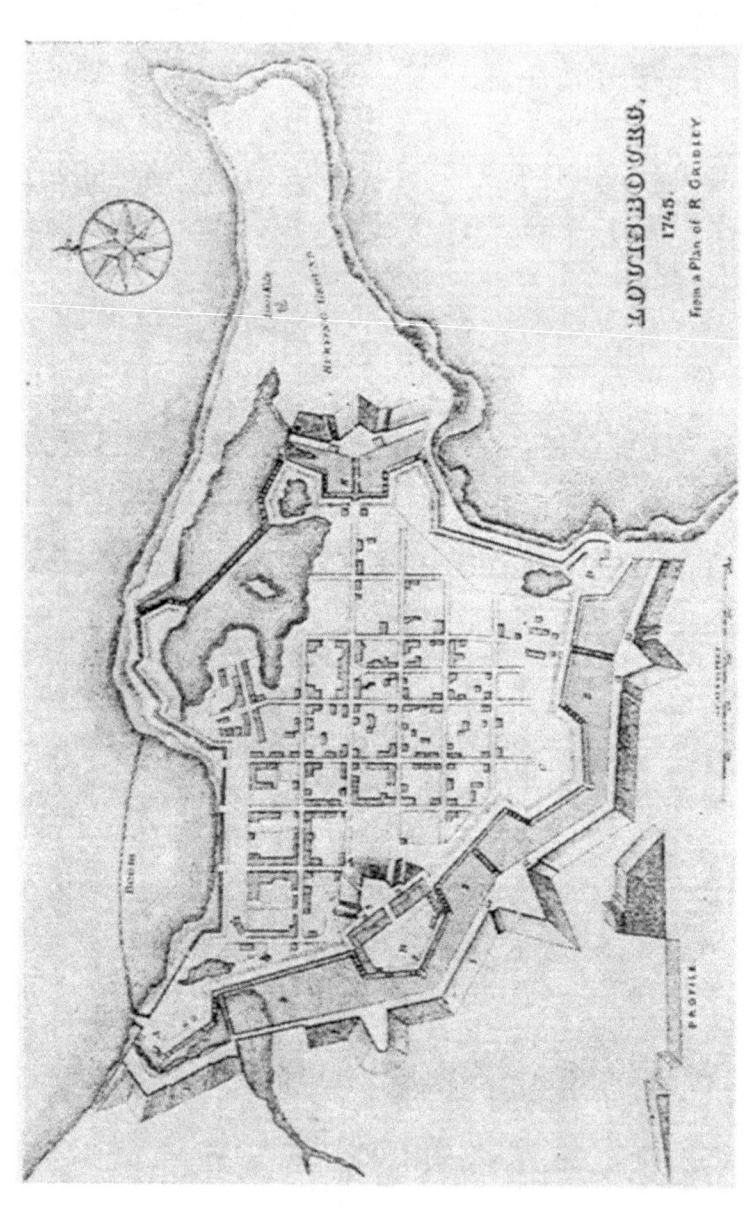

LOUISBOURG,
1745.
from a Plan of R. Gridley

INDEX

TO PLAN OF LOUISBOURG, 1745.

FROM A SURVEY BY LIEUTENANT-COLONEL R. GRIDLEY.

A Dauphin's Bastion and West Gate.
B King's Bastion, or Citadel.
C Queen's Bastion.
D Princess's Bastion and South Gate.
E Maurepas Bastion and East Gate.
1111 Glacis.
222 Ditch.

NEW HAMPSHIRE MEN IN THE LOUISBURG EXPEDITION, 1745.

NAMES.	Residence.	Enlisted.	Rank.	Company.	Reg't.
Atkinson, John.........		Feb. 13	Private	Moore's....	Moore's.
Ackers, Joseph	Exeter.........		"	Light's.....	"
Addison, Jonas			"	"	"
Atkinson, Joseph......	Brentwood		"	"	"
Adams, John..........	Londonderry..	June 20	"	Sherburne's	"
Ambrose, Jonathan....	Exeter		"	"	"
Aylmer, Valentine....			"	"	"
Abbott, Joseph........	Dover..........	Feb. 13	"	Hale's	"
Allen, Daniel..........	Greenland....		"	Whidden's.	"
Abbott, John..........			"	"	"
1 Allcock, John	Portsmouth....	Feb. 13	"	....	"
Arickson, Samuel......			"	"	"
Barker, John..........		Feb. 13	"	Moore's.....	"
Black, Adam		"	"	"	"
Blake, John, Jr.........	Kensington....	"	Corp.	"	"
1 Broughton, Noah	Portsmouth....	"	Private	"	"
Brown, Isaac..........		"	"	"	"
Batt, Thomas			Sergt.	Fellows's ..	"
Bell, Timothy			Private	"	"
Bickford, Jethro.......	Newington		"	"	"
Boothby, Jonathan....	Portsmouth....		"	"	"
Brewster, Richard....	"		"	"	"
Brown, Caleb	Brentwood		"	Light's.....	"
Brown, John	"		"	"	"
Boardman, John		Feb. 13	"	Sherburne's	"
Blake, Samuel	Kensington....		"	Prescott's..	"
Bean, Edward.........			"	Hale's	"
Bean, Nathaniel		Feb. 13	"	"	"
Berry, Joseph.........		"	"	"	"
2 Bunker, Benjamin	Durham.......	"	"	"	"
Buss, Joseph..........	Dover..........	"	"	"	"
Bussell, Jacob	"	"	"	"	"
Bussell, John	"	"	Sergt.	"	"
Blake, Timothy........	Hampton Falls	"	Private	Williams's.	"
Bond, Jonathan.......		"	"	"	"
3 Brown, Edmund	Hampton Falls	"	Ensign	"	"
Bennett, Abraham			Private	Whidden's.	"
Brewster, John			"	"	"
Barber, Joseph		April 15	"	Trefethen's	"
Blake, Josiah			"	"	"
Bassett, Richard......			"	....	"
Bean, Daniel	Kingston	Feb. 13	"	....	"
Bickford, Eleazer. ...	Durham.......	"	"	....	"
Blake, Samuel, Jr......	Kensington....		"	....	"
4 Blaster, Joseph.......			Mariner	....	"
Brooks, Edward	Portsmouth....	Feb. 13	Ensign	....	"
Buntin, Samuel			Private	....	"
Center, Abraham			"	Fellows's ..	"
Claridge, Thomas			"	"	"
Colbath, Pitman	Newmarket....		"	"	"
Colbath, Joseph			"	"	"
Colbath, Benjamin.....	Newington		"	"	"
Cooper, Jonathan			"	"	"
Cooper, John..........			"	"	"
Cloyd, James	Brentwood		"	Light's.....	"
Coney, Jack...........			"	"	"
Creighton, George.....	Exeter		"	"	"
Carter, John...........	Londonderry..	June 20	"	Sherburne's	"
Cass, Abner			"	"	"
Cotton, John	Portsmouth....	Feb. 13	Sergt.	"	"
Cunningham, Robert ..	Londonderry..	June 20	Private	"	"
Chapman, John	Kensington....		"	Prescott's..	"
Chase, Enoch			"	"	"

1 Taken prisoner.   2 Promoted to Ensign Aug. 10.   3 Promoted to Lieutenant
Oct. 1.   4 Killed.

NEW HAMPSHIRE MEN IN THE LOUISBURG EXPEDITION, 1745.—*Cont.*

NAMES.	Residence.	Enlisted.	Rank.	Company.	Reg't.
Challis, Thomas......		....	Private	Prescott's..	Moore's.
Choate, Jonathan......	Kingston	....	"	"	"
Clifford, William......	"	....	"	"	"
Cram, Benjamin		....	"	"	"
Cash, Thomas......	Dover..........	Feb. 13	"	Hale,s......	"
Clark, Josiah..........		....	"	"	"
Clark, Stephen......'.		....	"	"	"
Cook, Ebenezer......	Dover..........	....	"	"	"
Critchet, James......		....	"	"	"
Calfe, Robert..........	Chester......	....	Sergt.	Williams's.	"
Cass, Nason	Exeter......	....	Private	"	"
Cram, Daniel..........	Hampton Falls	....	"	"	"
Cucknet, William......		....	"	Whidden's.	"
Cummin, Benjamin		....	"	Trefethen's	"
Card, Edward..........	Newcastle	Feb. 13	Mariner	Fernald's ..	"
Card, Thomas..........	"	"	"	"	"
Colby, Spencer........	Portsmouth....	"	"	"	"
Crimble, Charles......		....	"	....	"
Carty, John		....	Private		"
1 Cass, Jonathan........	Kensington....	Feb. 13	"	....	"
Clark, Alexander	....	Oct. 17	Surgeon	....	"
Conner, Samuel........	....	Feb. 13	Lieut.	....	"
2 Cotton, Timothy.......	Portsmouth....	"	Private	....	"
Dalton, Benjamin.....	....	"	"	Moore's....	"
Dunkin, John	....	"	"	"	"
Dam, Jonathan	....	....	"	Fellows's ..	"
Downing, Joseph......	....	....	"	"	"
Dunn, Thomas	....	....	"	"	"
Dolloff, Amos	Exeter......	....	"	Light's....	"
Dolloff, David..........	"	....	"	"	"
Dudley, Joseph........	....	....	"	"	"
Dudley, Joseph, Jr.....	....	....	"	"	"
Davis, Moses..........	....	....	"	Prescott's..	"
Davis, William........	....	....	"	"	"
Dow, Charles	....	....	"	"	"
Dow, Nathan..........	Kensington....	....	"	"	"
Dam, William..........	Dover..... ..	....	"	Hale's	"
Daniels, David........	"	....	"	"	"
Drew, Zebulon........	"	....	"	"	"
Durgin, William		....	"	" ..	"
3 Dudley, Trueworthy..	Exeter........	Feb. 13	Capt.	Dudley's ..	"
4 Daniels, Eliphalet....	Durham.......	"	Lieut.	Fernald's ..	"
Doe, Daniel	"	....	Mariner	"	"
Daniels, Benjamin	....	Apr. 15	"	Trefethen's	"
Davison, Dudley......	....	"	"	"	"
Dam, George	Portsmouth....	Feb. 13	Private	....	"
Dam, Waymouth	....	"	"	....	"
Dam, Theophilus	Newington	Feb. 13	"	....	"
Dacker, David	Portsmouth....	"	"	....	"
Dearborn, Shubael	Hampton	....	"	....	"
Dent, John	Kingston	....	"	....	"
Denerson, John........	Portsmouth....	....	"	....	"
Dolloff, John	....	....	Sergt.	....	"
Dow, Jeremiah........	Hampton	....	Private	....	"
Downer, Andrew	....	....	Officer	....	"
5 Dudley, James........	Exeter........	Feb. 13	Lieut.	....	"
6 Dunn, Nicholas........	Portsmouth.....	"	Private	....	"
7 Emery, Anthony	Hampton	"	Surgeon	....	....
Elliot, Abraham.......	....	....	Private	Fellows's ..	Moore's.
Edgerly, John	....	....	"	Light's.....	"
Eslet, John............	....	....	"	Prescott's	"
Eastman, Samuel......	....	....	"	"	"
Evans, Stephen........	Dover	Feb. 13	"	Hale's	"

---

1 Died Sept. 13, 1745.   2 Taken prisoner.   3 Discharged July 21.   4 Wounded
and prisoner.   5 Discharged Aug. 7.   6 Killed.   7 Mass. Artillery Co.

3

NEW HAMPSHIRE MEN IN THE LOUISBURG EXPEDITION, 1745.—*Cont.*

Names.	Residence.	Enlisted.	Rank.	Company.	Reg't.
Ellest, John...........	....	....	Private	Williams's.	Moore's.
Emery, Daniel.........	....	....	"	Whidden's.	"
Edgerly, Samuel	Brentwood	Feb. 13	"	....	"
Eyre, John	Portsmouth....	"	Adjt.	....	"
Ficket, John	"	"	Private	Moore's....	"
1 Flagg, John...........	"	"	Lieut.	"	"
2 Flagg, John, Jr.......	"	"	Private	"	"
Forham, Richard	....	"	"	"	"
3 Fellows, Nathaniel....	....	June 20	Lieut.	Fellows's ..	"
Fitzgerald, Richard ...	....	....	Private	"	"
Foy, John	Dover.........	....	"	"	"
Furber, Richard	Newington	....	"	"	"
Ferrin, Moses...	....	....	"	Light's....	"
Fifield, William.......	....	....	"	"	"
Flanders, Moses	....	....	"	"	"
Folsom, Joseph	....	....	"	"	"
Forrest, John	....	....	"	"	"
Fellows, John........	....	....	"	Prescott's..	"
Ferrel, John...........	Somersworth..	Feb. 13	"	Hale's......	"
Folsom, John	"	"	"	"	"
Forse, John	Dover.........	"	"	"	"
Fowler, Morrice	"	"	"	"	"
Fox, Edward..........	Newmarket....	"	"	"	"
4 French, John	Hampton Falls	"	"	Williams's.	"
5 Fernald, John........	Portsmouth ...	"	Capt.	Fernald's..	"
Foss, Zachariah	....	"	Lieut.	"	"
Furbush, Benjamin....	Dover.........	....	Private	Wise's.....	"
Furguson, John.......	....	....	"	"	"
Fales, Nathan.........	....	....	"	....	"
6 Folsom, Jonathan :....	....	June 17	Lieut.	....	"
Frost, Samuel.........	Portsmouth ...	....	Private	....	"
Fullerton, William	Brentwood	....	"	....	"
Gooding, David.......	....	Feb. 13	"	Moore's....	"
Gordon, David........	....	"	"	" ...	"
Green, John..........	....	....	"	"	"
Gardner, Joseph......	....	....	"	Light's.....	"
Gibson, John.........	....	....	"	"	"
Giles, Joseph	Brentwood ...	....	"	"	"
Gilman, James........	....	....	"	"	"
Gordon, Robert.......	....	....	"	"	"
Gordon, James........	....	....	"	"	"
Gault, Adam	Londonderry .	June 20	"	Sherburne's	"
Gault, Patrick.........	"	"	"	"	"
Griffith, John, Jr.......	Portsmouth....	Feb. 13	Clerk	"	"
George, Joseph.......	....	....	Private	Prescott's..	"
Gilman, Joshua	....	... .	"	"	"
Gimpson, Thomas	....	....	"	"	"
4 Gove, Ebenezer.......	Hampton Falls	....	"	"	"
Gove, Joseph	" "	....	"	"	"
Green, Bradbury	....	June 17	Lieut.	"	"
Gerrish, William	Dover.........	Feb. 13	Private	Hale's	"
Giles, John...........	"	....	Corp.	"	"
Glidden, William	"	....	Private	"	"
Gorman, James	"	....	"	"	"
Gowell, John..........	"	....	"	"	"
Grace, Nicholas.......	"	....	"	"	"
Gray, Reuben........	"	....	Corp.	"	"
7 Gloster, John.........	Portsmouth....	Feb. 13	Private	Mason's ...	"
8 Goudy, James	....	"	"	"	"
Gardner, David.......	....	....	"	Whidden's.	"
Greeley, Peter........	....	....	"	"	"
Grove, John..........	....	....	"	"	"
Gale, Daniel..........	·	....	Officer	....	"

1 Promoted to Captain; no date. 2 Promoted Ensign July 9. 3 Promoted to
Captain Oct. 1. 4 Died. 5 Captain of the Sloop Abigail. 6 Died Jan. 20, 1746.
7 Negro Slave of Theodore Atkinson. 8 Killed.

NEW HAMPSHIRE MEN IN THE LOUISBURG EXPEDITION, 1745.—*Cont.*

NAMES.	Residence.	Enlisted.	Rank.	Company.	Reg't.
Gilman, Ezekiel........	Exeter........	Feb. 13	Major	....	Moore's.
1 Gilman, Robert........	"	"	Surgeon		"
Gilman, Jonathan......	Brentwood	April 15	Lieut.	....	"
Glidden, Charles.......	....	....	Private	....	"
Godfrey, Jonathan	Hampton......	Feb. 13	"	....	"
2 Hall, John............	....	....	"	Moore's....	"
2 Hall, Richard.........	....	....	"	"	"
Haley, Thomas........	....	....	"	"	"
Hodgdon, John........	....	....	"	"	"
Hodgdon, Israel.......	Newington	Feb. 13	"	"	"
Hunt, Abner...........	....	....	"	"	"
Huntress, Jonathan...	....	....	"	"	"
Huse, William.........	....	....	"	"	"
Ham, Jotham	....	....	"	Fellows's ..	"
Hooper, John.........	Portsmouth....	....	"	"	"
Huntress, Christopher.	Newington	Feb. 13	Ensign	"	"
Hutchins, John	....	....	Private	Prescott's..	"
3 Hale, Samuel	Portsmouth....	Feb. 13	Capt.	Hale's	"
Harris, Richard.......	"	"	Private	"	"
Hassam, Jacob........	Dover........	"	"	"	"
Ham, Clement........	"	"	Ensign	"	"
Hayes, Elisha....	"	"	Private	"	"
Heard, Samuel..... ...	"	"	Sergt.	"	"
Hill, Ichabod	"	"	Private	"	"
Holt, Charles	"	"	"	. "	"
Hubbard, John H......	"	"	Drum'r	"	"
Hurell, Gideon........	Portsmouth....	"	Private	"	"
Huntress, Samuel......	Dover........	"	"	"	"
Hussey, John.........	"	"	"	"	"
Harford, Nicholas.....	....	....	"	Wise's	"
Hall, John, Jr........	....	....	"	....	"
4 Ham, Joseph.........	Portsmouth....	Feb. 13	"	....	"
4 Ham, Weymouth.....	"	"	"	....	"
5 Ham, William	"	"	"	....	"
Hart, John	....	....	Lieut.	....	"
Hicks, John	Greenland....	Feb. 13	Private	....	"
5 Hilton, William.......	....	....	"	....	"
Hopkins, Edward......	Portsmouth....	"	"	....	"
Hutchins, George.....	"	Feb. 13	"	....	"
Ingalls, Peter.........	....	....	"	Williams's.	"
Jones, Thomas........	....	Feb. 13	"	Moore's....	"
Johnson, Thomas.....	....	....	"	Fellows's ..	"
Judkins, Joseph.......	....	....	"	Light's.....	"
1 Jackson, Joshua......	Portsmouth....	Feb. 13	"	....	"
Jackson, Elisha........	"	"	"	....	"
6 Jackson, Ebenezer	"	"	Sergt.	....	"
Johnson, Philip........	Greenland....	....	Private	....	"
Judkins, John.........	....	....	"	....	"
Keniston, Joseph.....	....	Feb. 13	"	Moore's....	"
Knight, Richard.......	....	....	"	Fellows's ..	"
Kelley, Daniel	....	....	"	Light's.....	"
Kennedy, Robert......	Londonderry..	June 20	Sergt.	Sherburne's	"
Kimball, Jonathan.....	....	....	Psivate	Prescott's .	"
Keniston, William.....	....	Feb. 13	"	Hale's	"
Kenney, Richard	....	"	"	"	"
Kenney, Love........	Dover........	"	"	"	"
Kinkett, David........	....	"	"	"	"
Keniston, Samuel, Jr..	Greenland.....	Feb. 13	Mariner	Fernald's..	"
Kimming, Benjamin...	Exeter	"	Officer	Dudley's'..	"
Keniston, Benjamin...	....	....	Private	Whiddens..	"
7 Keniston, John........	....	Feb. 13	Mariner	Fernald's...	"
Keniston, Samuel, Jr..	....	"	"	"	"
King, George	Portsmouth....	....	Artificer	....	....

1 Wounded.   2 Some places, written Hull.   3 Promoted to Major, Oct. 17, 1745.
4 Taken prisoner.   5 Died.   6 Wounded, and died.   7 Killed.

NEW HAMPSHIRE MEN IN THE LOUISBURG EXPEDITION, 1745.—*Cont.*

NAMES.	Residence.	Enlisted.	Rank.	Company.	Reg't.
Leary, Jeremy........	....	Feb. 13	Private	Moore's....	Moore's.
1 Loggin, John	....	"	"	"	"
Lamson, Nathaniel....	Exeter	....	"	Light's.....	"
Leary, Thomas........	....	....	"	"	"
Light, John	Exeter	June 17	Capt.	"	"
Lougee, Moses........	....	....	Private	"	"
Logan, Andrew........	Londonderry..	June 20	"	Sherburne's	"
Locke, Thomas	....	....	"	Prescott's..	"
Lowell, James	Hampton Falls	....	"	"	"
Libby, Benjamin......	Dover.........	Feb. 13	Sergt.	Hale's	"
Libby, Daniel	....	"	Private	"	"
Lowell, David........	....	....	"	Williams's.	"
Ladd, Daniel........	Exeter	Feb. 13	Capt.	Ladd's......	"
2 Ladd, Daniel, Jr......	"	"	Private	"	"
Ladd, John...........	....	June 17	Capt.	"	"
Leavitt, Jonathan	....	April 15	Private	Trefethen's	"
Leach, John..........	....	....	"	Wise's	"
3 Ladd, Jonathan, Jr....	Kingston	Feb. 13	Surgeon	....	"
Langdon, Samuel.....	Portsmouth...	Mar. 18	Chaplain	....	"
Lapish, William......	....	....	Private	....	"
3 Leavitt, Moses........	Hampton	Feb. 13	"	....	"
Leavitt, Joshua.......	....	....	"	....	"
Lewis, Benjamin......	Portsmouth....	Feb. 13	"	....	"
Libby, John	....	....	"	....	"
Leavitt, Samuel......	....	Feb. 13	Lieut.	....	"
4 Lufkin, Isaac	....	....	Private	....	"
Moore, Samuel........	Portsmouth....	Feb. 12	. Col.	Moore's....	"
Marston, William.....	....	Feb. 13	Private	"	"
Marston, James	....	"	"	"	"
Moulton, David.......	....	"	"	"	"
McMahone, Roger.....	....	....	"	Fellows's ..	"
Moore, Edward.......	....	....	Sergt.	"	"
Morgan, Andrew......	....	....	Private	"	"
Marcy, William.......	....	....	"	Light's.....	"
Marsh, James........	....	....	"	"	"
Moody, Clement......	Brentwood	....	"	"	"
5 Marston, Jeremiah....	Hampton	Feb. 13	"	Sherburne's	"
McLaughlin, John.....	Londonderry..	June 20	"	"	"
McLenchan, James....	"	....	"	"	"
McNeil, John..........	Manchester....	....	"	"	"
McNeil, James........	"	....	"	"	"
Miller, Samuel........	Londonderry..	....	"	"	"
Miller, John..........	"	....	"	"	"
3 Montgomery, Henry..	"	....	Ensign	"	"
6 Montgomery Hugh....	Portsmouth....	Feb. 13	Private	Prescott's..	"
Moulton, Henry.......	....	....	"	"	"
Moulton, Thomas......	....	....	"	"	"
3 Moulton, Simon......	....	....	"	"	"
Merrow, Samuel.......	Rochester	....	"	Hale's......	"
Marston, John	Hampton	....	"	Williams's.	"
Mason, John T.........	Portsmouth....	Feb. 13	Capt.	Mason's....	"
McGregor, Daniel.....	Londonderry..	June 20	"	McGregor's	"
Marston, Jonathan	....	....	Private	Whidden's.	"
Moulton, James	....	....	"	"	"
Marshall, Henry.......	Brentwood	April 15	"	....	"
Marshall, Hawley......	"	"	"	....	"
Martin, Michael.......	Portsmouth....	....	"	....	"
Martyn, Robert.......	"	....	"	....	"
Mason, Nathaniel.....	....	....	"	....	"
Mason, Benjamin.....	Hampton	....	"	....	"
Mason, Francis......	Stratham......	....	"	....	"
7 Mattoon, Richard.....	....	Feb. 13	Lieut.	....	"
Meader, Moses........	Durham.......	....	Private	....	"

1 Promoted to Ensign, July 16, 1745.   2 Taken prisoner.   3 Died.   4 Wounded.
5 Killed.   6 Killed.   7 Some places, Malloon.

NEW HAMPSHIRE MEN IN THE LOUISBURG EXPEDITION, 1745.—*Cont.*

NAMES.	Residence.	Enlisted.	Rank.	Company.	Reg't.
Merrill, Jacob..........	....	June 17	Ensign	....	Moore's.
Meserve, Nathaniel...	Portsmouth....	Feb. 13	Lt. Col.	Meserve's..	"
[1] Meserve, Nathaniel,Jr.	"	"	Lieut.	"	"
Meserve, George	"	June 20	Capt.	"	"
[2] Miller, Robert	Hampton Falls	Feb. 13	Private	....	"
Moody, John...........	....	....	"	....	"
Morgan, Abraham.....	Stratham	Feb. 13	"	....	"
[3] Morgan, John..	Kingston	"	"	....	"
Moulton, Nathaniel....	Hampton	....	"	....	"
[4] Newmarch, Thomas..	Portsmouth....	Feb. 13	Ensign	Fellows's ..	"
Norton, Caleb..........	....	....	Private	Prescott's..	"
Nute, Paul..............	Dover..........	April 15	"	Trefethen's	"
Nelson, Joseph	Portsmouth...	Feb. 13	"	Hale's......	"
Nelson, John..........	"	"	"	....	"
[5] Nelson, Leader........	"	"	"	....	"
Nelson, James	....	....	"	....	"
Peirce, Perham	....	Feb. 13	"	Moore's....	"
Perkins, George	....	"	"	"	"
Perry, John	....	"	"	"	"
Pinkham, John........	....	....	"	Fellows's ..	"
[6] Pitman, Ezekiel, Jr....	Portsmouth....	Feb. 13	Ensign	....	"
Philbrick, Joseph......	....	....	Private	Light's.....	"
[7] Prescott, William	Epping	Feb. 13	"	....	"
Palmer, Growth.......	"	"	"	Sherburne's	"
Page, David...........	Exeter	....	"	Prescott's..	"
[8] Prescott, Jonathan....	....	June 17	Capt.	"	"
Prescott, Joseph......	....	....	Private	"	"
[3] Prescott, John.... ..	Kingston	....	"	"	"
Pressey, Paul.........	"	....	"	"	"
Perkins, Thomas.......	Rochester	Feb. 13	Corp.	Hale's......	"
Perkins, Nathaniel	....	"	Private	"	"
Paine, John	Newcastle	....	"	Whidden's.	"
Peavey, Joseph.......	....	....	"	"	"
Partridge, Jonathan..	Portsmouth....	Feb. 13	"	....	"
Pease, Samuel.........	Newmarket....	....	"	....	"
Pendexter, Edward, Jr.	....	....	"	....	"
Perkins, Robert	....	Feb. 13	Ensign	....	"
Philbrick, Josiah......	....	Oct. 10	"	....	"
[3] Philbrick, Simon..... .	....	....	Private	....	"
Pickering, Thomas	....	Feb. 13	Ensign	....	"
Pierce, Joseph.........	Portsmouth....	Mar. 16	Sur. ch'f	....	"
Pinkham, Solomon	Dover..........	Feb. 13	Armorer	Light's......	"
Quimby, Eliphalet.....	....	....	Private	Light's.....	"
Rand, William........	Newcastle.....	Feb. 13	"	Moore's....	"
Randall, William	....	"	"	Fellows's ..	"
Rawlings, Stephen	....	"	"	"	"
Rawlings, Samuel.....	Newington	"	"	"	"
Read, Solomon........	Dover..........	"	"	"	"
Roberts, Isaac........	....	"	"	"	"
Rundlett, Satchel......	....	Feb. 13	"	Sherburne's	"
Robinson, Benjamin...	....	"	"	Light's.....	"
Rowe, Daniel	....	"	"	Prescott's..	"
Rowe, Nathan.........	Hampton Falls	....	"	"	"
Rowe, Robert	....	....	"	"	"
Richardson, Samuel...	....	....	"	Hale's	"
Ring, Eliphalet	Portsmouth....	Feb. 13	"	"	"
Roberts, Samuel.	Dover..........	"	"	"	"
Roberts, Thomas......	"	"	"	"	"
Rowell, Enoch.........	Chester	"	"	Williams's.	"
Rand, William, Jr... ..	....	....	"	....	"
[9] Rawlings, Joseph.....	Exeter.........	....	"	....	"
Read, Samuel.........	....	....	"	....	"
Redman, Joseph.......	Hampton	....	"	....	"

[1] Taken prisoner, Aug. 1, promoted to Lieutenant.   [2] Arm shot off.   [3] Died.
[4] Promoted to Lieutenant, Oct. 5, 1745.   [5] Taken prisoner.   [6] Promoted to Lieutenant, June 20, 1745.   [7] Lost a leg.   [8] Died April 12, 1746.   [9] Wounded, June 7.

NEW HAMPSHIRE MEN IN THE LOUISBURG EXPEDITION, 1745.—*Cont.*

NAMES.	Residence.	Enlisted.	Rank.	Company.	Reg't.
Roble, Samuel	Chester	Feb. 13	Lieut.	....	Moore's.
Robinson, Charles.....	....	....	Private	....	"
1 Sanborn, Abner.......	....	Feb. 13	"	Moore's....	"
Spriggs, William	....	"	"	"	"
Studley, William......	....	"	"	"	"
Senter, Abraham......	....	....	"	Fellows's..	"
Sherburne, Edward ...	....	....	"	"	"
Stevens, John..........	Newington ...	....	"	"	"
Sanborn, Josiah........	....	....	"	Lights'	"
Savage, Moses........	....	....	"	"	"
Scribner, Samuel.......	....	....	"	"	"
Severans, John	....	....	"	"	"
Sinkler, Ebenezer......	Exeter.........	....	"	"	"
Sinkler, Samuel.......	Stratham	....	"	"	"
Stockbridge, Abram...	Stratham	....	"	"	"
Sherburne, Henry	Portsmouth ...	Feb. 13	Captain	Sherburne's	"
Sherburne, Joseph....	"	June 6	"	"	"
Sherburne, Edward....	"	....	Private	"	"
Sims, Samuel..... ...	....	....	"	"	"
Stockbridge, Warren..	....	....	"	Prescott's..	"
Stevens, Ephraim......	....	....	"	"	"
Swain, William........	Hampton Falls	....	"	"	"
Sweet, Robert.........	....	....	"	"	"
Salter, Richard........	Dover........	....	"	Hale's	"
2 Sam..................	Portsmouth...	....	"	"	"
Sanborn, Marston.....	....	....	"	"	"
Smith, Archibald	Dover........	... .	"	"	"
Smith, John	....	....	"	"	"
Stanton, Benjamin. ...	Dover	Feb. 13	"	"	"
Stanton, Benjamin, Jr.	Somersworth..	"	"	"	"
Stoodley, Jonathan....	Portsmouth ...	....	"	"	"
Samborn, John..... ..	....	....	"	Williams's.	"
Samborn, Ebenezer....	....	....	"	"	"
Shaw, Benjamin.......	Hampton Falls	....	"	"	"
Seaward, William	So. Hampton..	Feb. 13	Captain	Seaward's .	"
Smith, James..........	....	....	Private	Wise's	"
Sleeper, Joseph........	Kingston	Feb. 13	Ensign	Ladd's	"
Sanborn, Shubael......	Hampton......	....	Private	....	"
Sargent, Nathaniel Jr.	"	Mar. 20	Surgeon	....	"
Shaw, Josiah..........	"	Feb. 13	Private	....	"
Sheafe, Jacob	Portsmouth....	Oct. 5	Comsy.	....	"
Sleeper, Moses........	Kingston	June 17	Lieut.	....	"
Sleeper, Henry	Portsmouth....	Feb. 13	Private	... .	"
Sleeper, John	Hampton	....	"	....	"
Studley, John	....	....	"	....	"
Thompson, Alexander.	....	Feb. 13	"	Moore's...	"
Tobey, Samuel........	....	"	"	"	"
Towle, Jabez..........	....	"	"	"	"
Treadwell, William E..	Portsmouth....	"	Comsy.	"	"
Turner, John..........	....	"	Private	"	"
Thompson, Samuel	....	....	"	Fellows's..	"
1 Thomas, John........	... .	Feb. 13	"	Sherburne's	"
Thompson, James	....	"	Corpl.	"	"
Thompson, William ...	Rochester	"	Private	Hale's	"
Titcomb, John	Dover.........	"	"	"	"
Tibbetts, Samuel......	"	....	Corpl.	"	"
Tilton, Benjamin......	Hampton Falls	.. ..	Private	Prescott's..	"
Taylor, James.........	....	....	"	Williams's.	"
Tilton, Jacob.........	Newmarket ...	Mar. 1	Captain	Tilton's	"
Trefethen, Abraham...	Newcastle.....	Apr. 15	"	Trefethen's	"
3 Tucker, Lewis	"	Feb. 13	Mariner	Fernald's..	"
Thing, Peter	Brentwood	....	Officer	....	"
4 Thomas, Benjamin	Portsmouth ...	Feb. 13	Private	....	"
Thompson, George....	"	....	"	....	"

1 Died.   2 An Indian.   3 Taken prisoner, died.   4 Wounded.

NEW HAMPSHIRE MEN IN THE LOUISBURG EXPEDITION, 1745.—*Cont.*

Names.	Residence.	Enlisted.	Rank.	Company.	Reg't.
[1] Thornton, Mathew.....	Londonderry..	Mar. 1	Surgeon	.. ..	....
Tilton, Daniel.........	....	....	Private	....	Moore's.
[2] Trefethen, Henry Jr...	Newcastle	Feb. 13	"	....	"
Trydick, Henry......	....	....	"	....	"
[3] Tufts, Thomas	....	Feb. 13	Ensign	....	"
[3] Veasey, Jeremiah......	....	June 17	"	Light's.....	"
Vittem, William	Hampton	Feb. 13	Private	Moore's....	"
[4] Vaughan, William.....	Portsmouth ...	"	Lt. Col.	....	
Vittem, William, Jr....	Hampton	"	Private	....	Moore's.
White, Nathaniel R....	Stratham	Feb. 13	Sergt.	Moore's....	"
Wilson, John....	....	"	Private	"	"
Wallace, Archibald....	....	....	"	Fellows's ..	"
Weare, Moses...........	....	....	"	"	"
Welch, John..	....	....	"	"	"
Wherrin, James	....	....	"	"	"
Wherrin, Isaac	....	....	"	"	"
Woodham, John	....	....	"	"	"
Waldron, Richard K...	Dover..........	Feb. 13	"	Hale's	"
Watson, Samuel	"	"	"	"	"
Wingate, Moses.......	"	"	Lieut.	"	"
Wingate, Daniel	"	"	Private	Light's....	"
Ward, James...........	....	....	"	"	"
Watson, Thomas......	....	....	"	"	"
Wells, John	....	....	"	"	"
Winslow, Joshua	.. ..	Sept. 30	Lieut.	"	"
Welch, David	....	....	Private	Sherburne's	"
Wright, Ebenezer	....	Apr. 15	Ensign	"	"
Ward, Daniel	....	.. ..	Private	Prescott's .	"
[5] Weare, Joseph.........	Kensington...	....	"	"	"
Weed, Joseph.........	....	....	"	"	"
[6] Worthen, Ezekiel......	Kensington ...	June 17	Ensign	"	"
Weare, Nathaniel......	Hampton Falls	....	Private	William's..	"
[2] Williams, Edward....	"	Mar. 2	Captain	"	"
Waldron, Thomas W..	Dover..........	Feb. 13	"	Waldron's .	"
Watson, Jonathan.....	Hampton Falls	....	Private	Ladd's......	"
Whidden, James......	....	Feb. 13	Captain	Whidden's.	"
Wise, John	....	Apr. 15	"	Wise's	"
Wood, James	....	Mar. 18	Sur.Mate	....	"
Wadleigh, Theophilus.	Epping	....	Private	....	"
Walden, John.........	....	....	"	....	"
Warren, Walter........	Portsmouth ...	....	"	....	"
Waters, Samuel.......	"	....	"	....	"
[1] Weymouth, Shadrick..	"	Feb. 13	"	... .	"
Wheelwright, Jeremiah	....	"	Lieut.	....	"
Whidden, Michael.....	Portsmouth ...	"	Private	....	"
Whidden, Nicholas....	....	"	Sergt.	....	"
White, Samuel........	....	"	Lieut.	....	"
Whitton, Samuel......	....	....	Captain	....	"
Wormall, Daniel	Brentwood	Feb. 13	Ensign	Hale's......	"
Young, Eleazer	Dover..........	"	Sergt.	Sherburne's	"
Young, Joseph........	....	....	Private	....	"
Yeatton, Philip	Somersworth..	Apr. 15	Ensign	....	"
York, Richard	Exeter.........	Feb. 13	Private	....	"
Young, Hezekiah......	Kingston	....	"	....	"

[1] Richmonds, Mass. Reg't. [2] Died. [3] Promoted to lieutenant Oct. 1, 1745. [4] Commissioned by Mass. [5] Promoted ensign Aug. 11, 1745. [6] Promoted to lieutenant Oct. 1, 1745. [7] Taken prisoner.

NEW HAMPSHIRE MEN IN THE LOUISBURG EXPEDITION, 1745.—*Cont.*

NAMES.	Residence.	Enlisted.	Rank.	Company.	Reg't.
Atherton, Philip			Private		
Bishop, Baly			Sergt.		
Blaucher, Edward			Private		
Braman, Thomas			Drum'r		
Campbell, Jeremiah			Private		
Caperon, John			"		
Cobb, Richard			Sergt.		
Crossman, Henry			Private		
Day, Edward			"		
Dorman, Micajah			"		
Esty, Benjamin			Sergt.		
Fillebrown, Thomas			Private		
Fisher, Nehemiah			Sergt.		
Fisher, Abijah			Private		
Fisher, John			"		
Fisher, Eleazer			"		
Forrest, John			"		
Forrest, Samuel			"		
French, Ephraim			"		
French, Jacob			"		
Glen, Richard			Corpl.		
Grover, Thomas			Private		
Hodges, Eliphalet			Corpl.		
Hodges, Benjamin			Private		
Hounestman, Heber			"		
Lane, Zepheniah			"		
Lyon, Elkanon			Clerk		
Napp, Aaron			Private		
Rogers, John			"		
Sheldon, Ephraim			"		
Thayer, Ephraim			"		
Thayer, Philip			"		
Tiffany, Joseph			Corpl.		
Tiffany, Robert			"		
Turner, Ebenezer			Private		
Weeks, John			"		
White, Abraham			"		
White, Daniel			"		
Wood, Benjamin			"		

[*Shirley to Wentworth.*]

Boston, March 4, 1745.

Sir,   As it will be uncertain where Mr Vaughan will be upon the arrival of this I am obliged to trouble you with 100^{lb} N. Tenour (by the bearer) to pay to those men, wch he shall have enlisted over & above the 150 to be aggregated to your Regiment, and to desire him to see y^t the men are march'd to Boston instantly to fill up the Incomplete Companies belonging te Colonel Hale's Regiment, wch will be there by the time those men get to Boston, or if he marches 'em to Charleston it will do : I must refer you for everything else at present to Mr Bastide, who will dine wth you on Monday—I am sorry I am obliged to trouble you wth the Letter wch accompanies this, at this improper time ; But I could not avoid, from the Importunity of the Council, and expectation of the assembly, doing it longer—I will write you further upon it by next post and must now subscribe my self in much haste and Truth

Your Exc^{ys} most obedient Humble servant

W. Shirley

His Exc^y Govr Wentworth

[The men referred to in the foregoing were raised in New Hampshire, over and above its own quota, to help Massachusetts fill its quota for the Louisburg expedition.   See Vol. V, 943.—Editor N. H. State Papers.]

From the above letter of Governor Shirley of Massachusetts it would appear that the thirty-nine men in the foregoing roll were from New Hampshire, but as it is uncertain, have put them in a separate roll.

THE CELEBRATION.

The *American Historical Register* has granted the writer permission to copy from its report of the proceedings at the celebration, in the July number for 1895, which he has done, in an abridged form.

THE LOUISBURG MONUMENT.

ERECTED BY THE SOCIETY OF COLONIAL WARS. UNVEILED JUNE 17, 1895.

The handsome marble column erected by the Society of Colonial Wars at Louisburg, Cape Breton, to commemorate the one hundred and fiftieth anniversary of the siege and surrender of the fortress of Louisburg to the New England troops under General Pepperell, was unveiled June 17. It was a successful event in every way. The weather was propitious to outdoor services and thousands of people from the surrounding country and from Halifax and Sydney, witnessed the function. Every State Society of Colonial Wars was represented, many members of the New York and New England Chapters were present on their private yachts with parties of friends.

The British war ship *Canada* was present and gaily decorated with bunting, as were the vessels in port and many private residences.

4

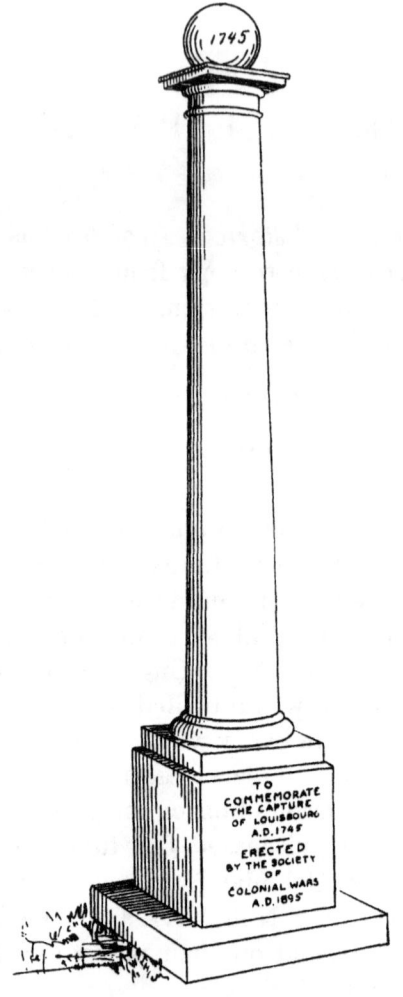

THE LOUISBURG MONUMENT.

The French Canadians entered heartily into the jollification, although the monument was to commemorate a victory over their ancestors Frequent mention was made by the speakers of the valor and chivalry of the French, and the hope was expressed that the French republic would always be on friendly relations with the United States and Great Britain. The land on which the monument is erected was donated by a Frenchman.

The assemblage was called to order at noon, in the King's Bastion of the ruins of the fortress, by the chairman of the Society's Monument Committee, Mr. Howland Pell, of New York, with some appropriate remarks. After prayer by the Rev. Dr. Salter, of Burlington, Iowa, the following address of Mr. Frederick J. de Peyster, of New York, governor-general of the Society, was read by Mr. Pell:

Mr. Governor, Gentlemen of the Society of Colonial Wars, and Guests: We have assembled here to-day among these storied ruins to dedicate the first—the very first—monument ever erected by the people of the Great Republic to commemorate the greatest triumph achieved by their colonial ancestors.

It is the greatest triumph, because it is the only instance recorded in history of the victory of a body of irregulars, led by a civilian, over well-trained and gallant foes. It was the success of shopkeepers, artisans, fishermen, farmers, and clerks commanded by a mere merchant, planned by a lawyer utterly ignorant of the art of war, over the regular soldiers of the first military power of Europe, led by well-trained, experienced, and gallant commanders, and intrenched within the strongest fortress of the New World.

The enterprise was a mad one, but it succeeded. Victory without the English fleet would have been impossible. The

English fleet was at first refused, but it arrived in good time
to complete the victory.   Thirty years ago, Goldwin Smith
said :

" The English yeomanry are no longer to be found in
England, the descendants of the brave youths who followed
the standards of Cromwell and Ireton no longer breathe
British air ; but they are not extinct; to-day you may find
them beneath the standards of Grant and of Sherman."

What renders this triumph of the Anglo-Saxon race the
more glorious is that it was won over worthy foes.   The
fortress which capitulated 150 years ago to-day was held
by the first soldiers of Europe, the warriors of the "Grand
Monarque."   Few laurels can be won by defeating a horde
of Asiatic slaves, but to tear the Lilies from the citadel was,
indeed, a splendid achievement.

The laurels won here were won from no poltroons, but
from the brave, romantic, chivalrous, but unfortunate children of glorious France.   The glory of this day is enough
for all.   Enough for English and American on the one hand
and the gallant soldiers of Louis on the other.   Both sides
were equally brave, but fortune, as usual, favored the big-
ger battalions.   Captain Mahan is right.   The true secret
of England's empire, of her long roll of victories, is her sea
power.   Had France instead of England controlled the sea,
French would be to-day the language of Boston, Philadel-
phia, and New York.   It was this long century of struggle
which decided the fate of the continent, and hence the
gratitude which we feel to those who battled so long, so
gallantly, and so successfully for the Cross of St. George.

Our Society of Colonial Wars is devoted to doing justice
to this very period, to the men who raised the scattered and
attenuated fringe of settlements along the Atlantic into the
mighty republic which is to-day the peer of the greatest
power on earth.   We wish that the unconquerable energy,
the heroic courage, the devoted patriotism of those earlier

days when Americans really became Americans, should remain the distinguishing characteristics of our race to the end of time.

And therefore we erect this monument to the memory of our heroic ancestors and as an inspiration to heroism for all generations of Americans.

Mr. Everett Pepperell Wheeler, of New York, one of the few living descendants of the hero of Louisburg, General Pepperell, and a member of the New York State Society of Colonial Wars, delivered the following oration of the day:

Mr. Governor, Gentlemen of the Society of Colonial Wars, and Guests: Heaven smiles on our undertaking. The northwest wind has driven away the clouds and fogs of the past week. Under the blue Cape Breton sky we commemorate achievements that, in their ultimate result, gave to the two great North American commonwealths their goodly heritage.

The Roman historian tells us that the leaders of his time used to say that when they looked on the statues of their ancestors their souls were stirred with a passion of virtue. It was not the marble, nor the features that in themselves had force. But the memory of their noble deeds kindled a flame in the breasts of their descendants which could not be quenched until their actions had equaled the renown and worth of their fathers.

In like manner we dedicate this monument in a spirit of gratitude to God and noble emulation for the heroism of man. No narrow spirit of local self-gratulation has brought us hither. We are glad to recognize that British sailors and colonial soldiers shared in the difficulties and dangers of the siege whose successful issue we celebrate to-day. And we are swift to acknowledge the courage and endurance of the garrison, who, cut off from succor and short of provisious, offered brave resistance for seven weeks to the British fleet and the regiments of Massachusetts, New Hampshire, and Connecticut.

In the Parliament of Quebec questions have been put to the government, indicating that the member who asked them thought that this monument was erected in the spirit of triumph over a fallen foe. To him I reply that we have not thus learned the lessons of history. This column points upward to the stars, and away from the petty jealousies that man the earth. It will tell, we trust, to many generations, the story of the courage, heroic fortitude, and manly energy of those who fought behind the ramparts, as well as of those who fought in the trenches. Some historians, it is true, have underrated the bravery of the defenders of the city, and even asserted that they surrendered before a breach was made in their walls, and when they might well have held out for months. The best answer to this is contained in an original document which gives the most authentic account of the siege: Governor Shirley's letter to the Duke of Newcastle. This was certified by Pepperell himself and by Waldo, Moore, Lothrop, and Gridley. It gives the following graphic description of the condition of the fortress when Du Chambon surrendered:

"And now, the Grand Battery being in our possession, the Island Battery (esteemed by the French the Palladium of Louisburg) so much annoyed from the Lighthouse Battery, that they could not entertain the hope of keeping it much longer; the enemy's northeast battery being damaged, and so much exposed to the fire from our advanced battery, that they could not stand to their guns; the circular battery ruined, and all its guns but three dismounted, whereby the Harbour was disarmed of all its principal batteries; the west gate of the city being demolished, and a breach made in the adjoining wall; the west flank of the King's Bastion almost ruined; and most of the other guns, which had been mounted during the time of the siege being silenced; all the houses and other buildings within the city (some of which were quite demolished) so damaged, that but one among them was left unhurt; the enemy extremely harassed by their long confinement within their casemates, and other covered holes, and their stock of ammunition being almost exhausted, Mr. Du Chambon sent out a flag of truce."

The men who stood in the trenches at Louisburg or dragged their cannon across its morasses were the best men of their colonies. They came hither inspired by no greed for conquest. Their expedition was really a defensive one. Their commerce had been assailed, their frontier settlements ravaged by hostile Indians, their wives and children massacred or carried into captivity. Louisburg was the harbor where the French privateers found refuge, and whence marauding expeditions sallied forth. Its massive walls were twenty-five years in building. Time has dealt hardly with these, but their ruins still bear witness to what was called at the time, the Dunkirk of America. The harbor which they covered you behold before you, landlocked and secure from the storms of this rockbound coast. The Island Battery and the Grand Battery barred all hostile entrance. And the city had magazines from which all Canada might be supplied.

The immediate occasion of the Louisburg expedition was an appeal for aid from Nova Scotia. In the archives of that province you will find a letter from Governor Mascarene to Governor Shirley, of Massachusetts. It was written at Annapolis Royall, December, 1744. In this your governor tells the story of the outbreak of war.

The honor of suggesting the Louisburg expedition has been claimed by several. Probably the thought occurred to more than one. The New England people were ripe for the attempt. Their state of mind at the time is well described by Belknap, the historian of New Hampshire:

" There are certain latent sparks in human nature which, by a collision of causes, are sometimes brought to light, and, when once excited, their operations are not easily controlled. In undertaking anything hazardous, there is a necessity for extraordinary vigor of mind and a degree of confidence and fortitude which shall raise us above the dread of danger and dispose us to run a risk which the cold maxims of prudence would forbid. The people of New England have at various times shown such an enthusiastic ardor, which has been excited by the example of their ancestors and their own exposed situation. It was never more apparent, and perhaps never more necessary, than on occasion of this expedition. Nor ought it to be forgotten that several circumstances, which did not depend on human foresight, greatly favored this undertaking."

The General Court of Massachusetts decided, on January 29, by a majority of one vote, to undertake the expedition. Immediately preparations were made with the utmost speed. Those who had opposed the plan, because of its danger, vied with its supporters in activity to promote its success.

It is not surprising that the enterprise should have aroused the enthusiasm of men like the colonists of that day. They were the most resolute and fearless of a resolute and fearless race. Religious zeal had led some to this country. Love of adventure had influenced others. They were inured to hardship by constant struggle with nature. They had built their own houses and their own ships, had cleared forests and ploughed fields.

The exigency of their situation had made them ready for any emergency. There were few factories in America, and the necessaries of life were largely supplied by the industry of the hamlets. The embroidered waistcoats and purple coats of the gentry, as you see them in the portraits of Copley and Smybert, came from home, as England still was called. But the garments of the sailors and farmers, who battered down the walls of Louisburg, were woven around their firesides in the long winter evenings.

And then we must remember that the people of the thirteen colonies were a commercial and seafaring people. They dwelt in a narrow strip of land extending along the Atlantic coast.

Thus have I tried to sketch the characteristics of the Americans of 1745. In times of peril such characteristics always find embodiment in a leader. It is common and easy to say that great men are but the expression of their time and lead it only in the sense that the spray leads the billow. That is but half the truth. When God gives to mankind the inestimable gift of a great man, he does, it is true, represent the spirit of his age. But he leads it, as the moon does the tides. Happy the people who appreciate such a man and are filled by his spirit, as the Bay of Fundy in every creek and inlet is filled by the advancing flood. It was fortunate for the colonies that in the emergency of 1745 there was a leader whom they trusted, and who was wise enough to discard the visionary schemes of others; brave enough to face the veterans of France, intrenched behind the walls which the skill and experience of Vauban had planned, and self-sacrificing enough to leave home and business, and all that made life pleasant and sweet, to endure the hardship and peril of this expedition, which Parkman calls "a mad scheme"—but which Pepperell and his followers dared to undertake.

I could not do justice to the occasion or the subject if I failed to speak for a moment of his remarkable career. He was a notable instance of the versatility and adaptiveness which the life of those days compelled. He was a successful merchant. He was a gallant soldier, accustomed from early youth to draw the sword in defense of his home and country. He had been in actual service against the In-

dians before he was twenty-one. It might have been said
of him, as it was of Wolfe, that he,

> Where'er he fought,
> Put so much of his heart into his act,
> That his example had a magnet's force,
> And all were swift to follow, whom all loved.

He was for twenty-nine years chief justice of the Court
of Common Pleas for Maine. He was an active and con-
spicuous member of His Majesty's Council for the colony
of Massachusetts. It is but just to him to add that his
religion was not disfigured by bigotry or intolerance. It
was an evident power in his life, but it always respected
the religion of others.

And now let me return to the story of the expedition
itself. I will not dwell upon its details. Representatives
of societies from various states have spoken of what each
colony did to promote its success. Massachusetts (which
then included Maine) certainly did the most. She was
the richest and most populous. But New Hampshire and
Connecticut did much, and New York, New Jersey, Rhode
Island, and Pennsylvania came forward to aid, though no
troops of theirs were in the trenches. A Rhode Island
sloop of war rendered essential service.

When we remember how difficult communication between the colonies was at the time of which we are speak-
ing, we shall wonder that they acted so much in concert—
not that they did no more. The mails were infrequent—
roads were poor. Oftentimes the travelers in a stage
coach were obliged to get out and lift the wheels out of
the mud in which they sunk to the hubs. No one had
even dreamed of railroad or electric telegraph. The won-
derful power of steam was unknown. It will help us to
realize the obstacles which beset any concerted action on
the part of the colonies when we remember that even in
the old mother country roads were so bad, and the trans-
mission of intelligence so slow, that the Chevalier had

been in Scotland nearly three weeks before the news reached Edinburgh. The tidings of the surrender of Louisburg did not reach Boston until July 3, sixteen days after the event, and were first known in New York a week later.

Such were the difficulties that our fathers had to face. Yet, withal, they had encouragement. Providence had favored their cause. The harvest of 1744 had been abundant, the winter was mild, the frontiers of New England had been unmolested, unexpected supplies arrived from Great Britain. The Grand Battery was not well fortified on the land side. The city had deprived itself of provisions to furnish the East India fleet and squadron for its recent voyage to France, and the *Vigilante*, which brought supplies, was captured by Warren. The weather during the siege was generally fine. The colonial troops captured in the Grand Battery, and fished up at the careening basin, the heavy cannon which they needed.

But all these would have availed nothing had it not been for the courage, the perseverance, the aptitude of the men who took advantage of these favoring circumstances, and brought their fleet of 100 vessels, with the little army of 4,050 men, safely to Canseau. There, to their great delight, on April 23, appeared Warren's squadron. Thence they sailed to Louisburg; on April 30, the troops landed, and after seven weeks of toil and peril, diversified, as we learn, when the soldiers were off duty, by games and sports, the fortress was theirs.

Their hardihood and daring are described in the words of one of the gallant French garrison as repeated by Gibson in the journal before-mentioned:

" This gentleman, I say, told me that he had not had his clothes off his back, either by night or day, from the first commencement of the siege. He added, moreover, that in all the histories he had ever read, he never met with an instance of so bold and presumptuous an attempt; that 'twas almost impracticable, as any one could think, for only three or four thousand raw, undisciplined men to lay siege to such a strong, well-fortified city, such garrisons, batteries, etc. For should any one have asked me, said he, what number of men would have been sufficient to have carried on that very enterprise, he should have answered not less than thirty thousand. To this he subjoined that he never heard of or ever saw such courage and intrepidity in such a handful of men, who regarded neither shot nor bombs. But what was still more surprising than all the rest, he said, was this, namely, to see batteries raised in a night's time, and more particularly the Fascine battery, which was not five-and-twenty rods from the city wall; and to see guns that were forty-two pounders dragged by the English from their grand battery, notwithstanding it was two miles distant, at least, and the road, too, very rough."

The tidings of the surrender were received throughout the colonies with the utmost enthusiasm. The contemporary accounts are too graphic not to be quoted:

" Now the churl and the niggard became generous, and even the poor forgot their poverty, and in the evening the whole town (Boston) appeared, as it were, in a blaze, almost every house being finely illuminated."

And now, let us pause for a moment and ask what was the result of this expedition. Do its consequences merit a monument? At first sight, apparently not. The capture of Louisburg is one of those historical events which was fruitful of great results, but which, for the most part, are slow in germination. Immediately it secured the cod fishery to the colonists for three years; it cut the French fishermen off from the Banks for a like period; it destroyed the French Atlantic trade for 1745; it gave the English a

prize which enabled them to buy back Madras at the treaty
of Aix la Chapelle. India was more valuable in the eyes
of the Duke of Newcastle than all the Atlantic colonies.

But the remote consequences of this expedition far trans-
cend in importance these immediate ones. It was a school
of arms for the colonial troops. Gridley, who planned the
parallels and trenches at Louisburg, laid out also the fortifications of Bunker Hill.

Its success showed the colonies their power and the
necessity for their union. It showed them, too, that in the
councils of Great Britain their affairs were of minor importance. This was a dreadful shock to the loyal love of
the old home which then was general in the colonies. On
the other hand, the capture of Louisburg pointed out to
William Pitt the possibility of the conquest of the whole of
Canada, and paved the way for that.

In the next war Canada was conquered, and the English
colonists freed from the fear of attack from their neighbor
on the north. The expenses of this war and the consequent
demands of the British exchequer, led the ministry to tax
the colonies. America resisted, and the result was the
American Revolution. By an extraordinary turn in the
wheel of time, the French assisted the old English colonies
to become an independent nation, while the old French
colonies remained the property of Great Britain.

It is now one hundred and fifty years since the surrender
of Louisburg. It is one hundred and twelve years since
the treaty of Paris recognized the independence of the
United States and confirmed to Great Britain the possession
of Canada. Surely the rancor of the old wars ought by
this time to be burned completely out. Surely we can now
agree that the development of these countries during all
that time has been promoted by the result of those old
wars. And despite, perhaps partly in consequence of, the
magnitude and costliness of the fleets and armies of to-day,
we may believe that the ties of Christian faith, the links of

mutual trade, the bands of friendship, the swift steamer, and the swifter electric current have bound us so closely together that English and French and American armies shall never more meet on the battlefield. We vie in the peaceful contests of art and science, and will settle the inevitable disputes by arbitration. There are social problems before us, as difficult of solution as any that have vexed the past. The very complication of the interlacing nerves of our modern civilization, which offers so many obstacles to war and binds nations over to keep the peace, is producing disorders and dangers within each state that require nicer surgery than that of the sword or the bayonet.

It is then with faces to the future that we dedicate this monument to the memory of all the brave men who fought and fell at Louisburg, whether under the Cross of St. George or the Lilies of France. The morning sun will illumine its summit. The sunset ray will gild its massive and simple outline. The storms and fogs of Cape Breton will gather round it. In sunshine and storm alike, let it tell to all mankind that peace has her victories, no less renowned than war; that the courage and resolution of the fathers live in the hearts of their children ; that we are prepared to face the conflicts, the difficulties and the perils of the coming century in firm reliance upon the protecting care of the same God who was with our fathers and will be with all who are loyal to Him to the end of time.

Addresses were also made by Dr. Mackay of the N. S. Historical Society, D. H. Ingraham, United States consul-general for Nova Scotia, and representatives of the various State Societies of Colonial Wars, when the monument was unveiled by His Honor Lieutenant-Governor Daly of Nova Scotia, on behalf of His Excellency the Earl of Aberdeen, governor-general of Canada; and salutes were fired.

After benediction by the Rev. T. Fraser Draper, rector of St. Bartholomew's Church, Louisburg, the members of the Society of Colonial Wars and their guests dined together.

In the evening, at the Sydney hotel, the mayor and recorder of Sydney and warden of the municipality presented an address of welcome, congratulation, and thanks to the visiting members of the Society of Colonial Wars. Happy responses were made by several of the visitors and by A. G. Jones, and a very pleasant time was brought to a close by singing "Auld Lang Syne."